T0340026

Digital Supply Chain Leadership

Strong leadership is necessary to drive the transformational change required to build and apply digital capabilities across organizations. Digital transformation in the supply chain is a leadership problem first and foremost. This book draws out some of the key digital business strategies supply chain leaders must become familiar with as they take on the responsibilities of leading transformations within their firms.

The central rationale of the book is to establish a clear business case for the performance shifts and opportunities of the digital supply chain. The benefits of a digital supply chain for firms can be summarized as uniquely reducing the amount of trade-off between costs and customer satisfaction. The challenges, complexity, and management involved in transforming to a digital supply chain have slowed many firms in their implementation. The key to unlocking this value and advantage is a new, robust, and digitally aware supply chain leadership mindset. It will provide readers with a practical digital supply chain leadership road map that will accelerate actions in technology, analytics, talent, and business models. The road map to digital transformation will step the reader through these critical dimensions and illustrate how they can support their own organizational transformation by developing greater levels of maturity.

This book will be most valued by supply chain leaders in medium to large-scale organizations, as well as consultants and academics interested in digital business and supply chain transformation. The book will also be valuable for students studying digital transformation, supply chain, and operations.

David B. Kurz is Associate Clinical Professor in the Management Department of Drexel University's LeBow College of Business, USA.

Murugan Anandarajan is Professor of MIS at the LeBow College of Business at Drexel University, USA.

Routledge Studies in Leadership Research

Digital Supply Chain Leadership

Reshaping Talent and Organizations

David B. Kurz
and Murugan Anandarajan

NEW YORK AND LONDON

First published 2021
by Routledge
52 Vanderbilt Avenue, New York, NY 10017

and by Routledge
2 Park Square, Milton Park, Abingdon, Oxon, OX14 4RN

Routledge is an imprint of the Taylor & Francis Group, an informa business

Library of Congress Cataloging-in-Publication Data
A catalog record for this title has been requested

ISBN: 978-0-367-26317-1 (hbk)
ISBN: 978-0-367-71643-1 (pbk)
ISBN: 978-0-429-29255-2 (ebk)

Typeset in Sabon
by MPS Limited, Dehradun

Contents

List of Figures and Table

Figure

Table

Preface

In April 2020, a radio journalist contacted Drexel University to inquire if anyone could do an interview on the topic of supply chains. A few emails later, my colleague and I were in touch and informed him we were writing a book on this very topic. The previous evening, one of the cable news programs devoted an entire segment of its show to the supply chain. Supply chains were in the news, maybe in a way they had never been before, though it wasn't hard to think of reasons why. Critical shortages of personal protection and lifesaving equipment needed for frontline medical personnel fighting the disastrous spread of the Coronavirus/COVID-19 were tragically evident, with the impacts creating terrifying headlines. Of lesser importance, yet highly visible, were images of empty grocery store shelves and frustrated consumers. The radio journalist began by asking us questions such as "What is the supply chain?" and "How has the supply chain changed due to Coronavirus/COVID-19?" These and all the questions in-between made us think, and rethink, many of the concepts covered in this book.

The journalist told us that he had never given much thought to the supply chain, or what it was made up of, because prior to the Coronavirus/COVID-19, most supply chains just worked. When supply chains are working reasonably well, they are invisible to the end consumers of many products. The items we wanted or needed were simply there on the store shelf, or one click away from an online retailer, ready for immediate shipping. It's "almost like magic" I told the journalist, explaining how the things we need are available and how people become mildly annoyed when goods are occasionally out of stock or delayed. A great supply chain shouldn't be taken for granted and the best supply chains in the world have constantly invested to become better and better at forecasting demand for products, and at being able to produce them at a quality that meets or exceeds customer expectations while delivering them into the hands of consumers exactly when they want them. They are complex systems that are much more global, integrated, and networked among business partners than most of the general population realize.

The second big question dealt with whether or not the supply chain had changed as a result of the Coronavirus crisis. While it may be too early to say as of this writing, it appears that certain aspects of supply chains, and how they are managed, will change in the foreseeable future. The biggest shift may be in mindset. One of the most mission-critical metrics for supply chain leaders has always been managing cost, particularly in inventories as holding inventory is not a cost-free decision. Much of the supply chain literature and research has focused on minimizing supply chain cost while attempting to satisfy customer demand. The promise of the digital supply chain, which is the focus of this book, is to find ways to meet both of these, at times divergent, goals concerning low costs and high customer satisfaction. Digital supply chains have shown that they may be able to move this trade-off curve between cost and demand satisfaction, something supply chain leaders have struggled with mightily for decades.

While many things have, or will have, changed, there are undoubtedly some things that will not. Several years ago, before the term digital supply chain came to be widely used, we observed numerous global firms developing strategies to become more "end-to-end" supply chains (Payne, 2019). They talked about integration across functions, and tighter connections with value chain partners. Technology was mentioned, albeit without quite envisioning the extent to which it is available now. What was universal, and unrelated to any particular time, technology or event, was the need for leadership.

Supply chains in most firms are complex organisms (Wieland et al., 2016). They have many dependencies across varying internal functions, as well as across external partner firms. To initiate change, from the more modest functional change to enterprise transformational change, requires executives and managers to take leadership action. In our research with supply chain leaders from around the world, there is a consensus that strong supply chain leadership is needed. This book serves as a guide for those leaders.

References

Payne, T. (2019). *Leverage Gartner's Digital Supply Chain Planning Maturity Model to Improve Planning Quality. Gartner research note*, July 2019.

Wieland, A., Handfield, R., Durach, C. (2016). Mapping the Landscape of Future Research Themes in Supply Chain Management. *Journal Of Business Logistics*, 37(3), 205–212.

Acknowledgments

Dave would like to extend a big thanks to Chris Caine, President of the Center for Global Enterprise, which has for the last several years sponsored the Digital Supply Chain Institute (DSCI). Chris asked me to participate in the DSCI research activities which has been a wonderful opportunity, and which undoubtedly has inspired numerous ideas in this book. Thanks to the entire staff of the Institute including Vivek Ghelani, Ira Sager, Shawn Muma, Sugathri Kolluru, and Monica Consiglio. Also, very special thanks to George Bailey, the Executive Director and Chief Research Officer of the DSCI, as well as Craig Moss, Managing Director of DSCI and Senior Partner at Ethisphere. George, Craig and, I collaborated extensively throughout 2017 on one of our first papers on Digital Supply Chain Metrics, where the initial ideas for this book began to emerge through countless hours of discussion. George and Craig's work are very evident in the two Appendixes on Metrics and the Transformation Assessment tool. They graciously agreed to allow those tools to be published here. Thanks also to Murugan for his terrific support for many years in my work at Drexel LeBow.

About the authors

Professor David B. Kurz is an expert on organizational learning and leadership development. His research and practice focuses on improving collaborative performance enabling effective strategy execution. Dr. Kurz advises global organizations on innovative learning and leadership development strategies. His research covers organizational behavior topics such as leadership, team performance, and enabling digital value chain transformation. Dr. Kurz has worked on performance improvement projects for a wide range of industries and clients covering technical, process, and human capital perspectives. His experience spans global organizational cultures in North and South America, Europe, Asia, and Africa.

Dr. Kurz currently holds a faculty appointment as an associate clinical professor in the management department of Drexel University's LeBow College of Business, where he is a leader in developing the school's capabilities in experiential learning. Dave has previously served as a Principal and Vice President of Learning Design for the critically recognized education and strategy firm CorpU. Additionally, he has lectured at the University of Pennsylvania, has lead experiential programs for Wharton Executive Education, and has delivered invited talks on organizational learning strategy at the ATD Global Congress. He was a featured speaker at the e-Learning 3.0 conference and has moderated a panel on learning technology in business at the World Economic Forum. He is the author of "Leading the Digital Supply Chain" featured in the Routledge publication entitled *The Internet of People, Things and Services: Workplace Transformations*. He is also the coauthor of *The Digital Supply Chain Transformation Guide: Essential Metrics*, published by the Digital Supply Chain Institute and the primary author of *Talent & Organizational Planning: A Guide to Closing the Digital Supply Chain Skills & Performance Gap*.

Dr. Kurz is a fellow of the *Institute for Strategic Leadership* at Drexel LeBow and a research fellow for the *Digital Supply Chain Institute*, a non-profit think tank based in New York City. He holds Masters and Doctoral degrees from the University of Pennsylvania.

Murugan Anandarajan, PhD is a professor of MIS at the LeBow College of Business at Drexel University. He is the head of the Department of Management as well as the Department of Decision Sciences and MIS.

His research expertise intersects the areas of Crime, Internet of People, Things and Service (IoPTS), and Analytics. Much of his recent work has focused on cybercrime in Medical IoT, and impact of digital technologies on business. He has published over fifty articles in peer-reviewed journals, including *Decision Sciences, Journal of MIS, Journal of International Business Studies* and *Communications of the ACM* among others. He has served in editorial positions for several academic journals; and has presented at many academic conferences and seminars. Murugan has won numerous awards for his research including outstanding researcher award from the LeBow College of Business in 2003 and 2004.

Murugan has co-authored eight books, including *Internet and Workplace Transformation* (2006) and its follow up volume, *The Internet of People, Things and Services* (2018). Forthcoming books include *Aligning Business Strategies and Analytics: Bridging Theory and Practice* (2018) and *Practical Text Mining: A Content Analysis Perspective to Maximize the Value of your Text Data* (2018). His observations and research have been cited in the media, including CNN, CBS News, ABC, and WMAR, Wired Magazine, CIO, and Philadelphia Business Journal among others.

He has been awarded over $2.5 million in research and pedagogy grants to support his research from various government agencies including the National Science Foundation, U.S. Department of Justice, National Institute of Justice, and the State of PA as well as organizations, such as SAP America, Lockheed Martin, Accenture, and Bristol Meyers.

Murugan has developed numerous programs at LeBow, including the Technology and Innovation Management and Organizational Management, both undergraduate co-majors in the Department of Management as well as the graduate programs in Supply Chain Management and Logistics and the forthcoming Business Analytics (online) both in the Decision Sciences Department. He was instrumental in the development of the Executive DBA in 2017. Murugan has taught and developed numerous courses at the undergraduate, graduate, doctoral levels as well as been involved in executive education.

In addition to his teaching, Murugan is heavily involved in undergraduate research through the Students Tackling Advanced Research (STAR) Scholars Program, which encourages first-year students to participate in faculty-mentored research. He has trained these undergraduates in qualitative research methods since 2005. In 2014, Drexel honored him with the STAR mentor of the year award.

Murugan, cofounded the Analytics 50, an annual event which recognizes the top 50 analytics executives leading innovative in analytics solutions for business challenges. Previous winners include GE, North face, Citrix, Comcast, Toyota, Philadelphia 76ers, Mercy Health among others.

He serves as the academic director of the Business Analytics Solution Center. Through the center he has led students in consulting projects with companies such as SEI, Children's Hospital of Philadelphia, Dow Chemical, and Pfizer among others.

Murugan received his doctorate in MIS from the Drexel University in 1997.

1 What is the Digital Supply Chain?

Closing the Performance Gap

Business transformations enabled by technology are not a new phenomenon. For decades, advances in manufacturing, distribution, and information technologies have offered opportunities for businesses to reduce costs while improving their products, managing their distribution, and understanding their customers better. In the modern era, ERP systems, such as SAP, PeopleSoft, and Oracle, have promised users more integrated, enterprise control of their business operations, and launched numerous "transformation" projects in firms to implement them. Similarly, the growth of the internet also created opportunities and challenges for firms seeking to remain competitive while taking advantage of new business models enabled by greater connectivity with trading partners and customers. Businesses are now faced with a new chapter in the technological change continuum in the growth of digital business models. As we are now in the midst of this particular change, it is critical to understand what is meant by "digital" business, how it differs from traditional business models, and, subsequently, how we can lead our organizations through the key dimensions of the new models.

Like many business disciplines, supply chain management has hosted a succession of popular theories prompted by industry analyst researchers and forward-thinking leaders that are discussed and sometimes acted upon. As supply chain ERP projects in many firms began to be augmented by web-enabled applications, such as Ariba, serious thinkers dedicated to supply chain performance improvement began speaking of an "end-to-end" supply chain referring to a more integrated supply chain that designed and accounted for a broader range of a business partner's interests, such as suppliers, third-party logistics firms, and customers and consumers. Supply chain leaders, not content to simply focus on functions and performance in-house, were enabled by new online forms of communications to build a broader chain of interrelated partners and customers. Large, global supply chain leaders were beginning to speak of end-to-end supply chain transformations in their firms, signaling the desire for a larger-than-incremental need for change. End-to-end supply chain integration requires a greater degree of fluidity of data and information sharing, both internally as well as external to the firm. The "Digital Supply Chain" (DSC) started gaining traction as a distinct term around the midpoint of the previous decade (Michel, 2017). In many ways, the shift to DSC was, in reality, the technological enablement of a more end-to-end supply chain. Digital tools, processes, and the resulting data were the glue that allowed for the construction of the upstream and downstream supply chain actors and their activities. Digital information is an essential ingredient to fueling end-to-end business integration. More significantly, businesses that can shift to DSCs are discovering that they may unlock performance improvements previously unreachable by traditional methods. Digital transformation is a shift, a change to new ways of operating (AE Consultancy, 2015). It requires changes in business models and the innovative use of technology to improve the experiences of your value chain partners and your customers (AE Consultancy, 2015).

Arguments in support of digital business transformation abound and some benefits which have been elaborated on include; increased revenues, lower costs to produce and deliver products, increased competitive advantage, customer satisfaction improvements, amongst others (Bui, 2019). For supply chain leaders, the cited benefits of a DSC are especially exciting, as they offer a potential way of overcoming a most perennial operational trade-off: the balance between inventory holding costs and being able to quickly satisfy customer demand. DSCs offer a potential pathway to shifting the trade-off paradigm while allowing for both conditions, existing previously in direct conflict, to be met simultaneously (Figure 1.1).

Figure 1.1 illustrates the cost savings and performance improvement potential when investing in DSC strategies and actions. Supply chain leaders have always struggled with a core dilemma: the inevitable trade-off between customer satisfaction and the cost of delivering it. Supply chain leaders know that inventory is not free and that maintaining overly high levels of safety stocks is costly for the firm. Inventory holding costs, damage, and obsolescence, have historically been some of the most keenly managed and measured of all supply chain performance metrics. Many supply chain leaders recognize that the single most important metric they manage is inventory turns realizing that this metric cascades directly to a firm's overall financial and operational performance. At the same time, however, firms are competing to earn customer trust, loyalty, and satisfaction. Customers want and often expect on-time in-full (OTIF) delivery. The easiest way to ensure OTIF is to fill warehouses full of products so that orders can be immediately shipped once they come in. This is not the reality most firms are facing. OTIF is a moving target stabilized by keenly managed inventories and

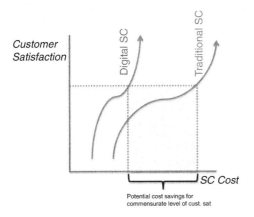

Digital Supply Chain Cost Saving Potential
Reducing the trade-off between Customer Satisfaction and Costs

Figure 1.1 DSC Performance Increase Potential.

low-cost transportation. In the best firms, these two completing demands are considered trade-offs, a kind of optimal curve where few
business options are available to make significant improvements in either dimension. Figure 1.1 illustrates a DSC opportunity with each
curve being a function consisting of a sampling of key performance
measures. For customer satisfaction, factors such as OTIF, Net
Promoter Score (a proxy for customer satisfaction), and some net
growth in orders might be measured to indicate how well a firm is doing
in meeting customer needs and expectations. On the supply chain cost
side, the all-important inventory holding costs are measured, as well as
transportation costs, the cost of stock outs, and the added costs of
manufacturing required to meet customer demands. This equation,
again as proxies, suggests that when it comes to satisfying a valued
customer planning must be carried out properly, otherwise firms might
face emergency transportation costs for expediting goods, and if forecasts have been calculated poorly, firms might run out of stock leading
to ramifications far beyond the simple loss of current sales. Increased
manufacturing costs may arise from an unexpected changeover of a
production line needed to produce additional product exceeding the
forecasted demand. Added together, these curves represent a functional
amalgamation of these integrated factors. Looking at the Traditional
Supply Chain curve, on the right side of the chart, we can imagine an
upward slope of costs that roughly tracks increases in customer satisfaction. These curves will likely be very different by product segment
and customer. For the purposes of this visualization, let's assume we are
looking at one product segment of one firm. The argument in favor of a

DSC is that digital actions, emerging from investments in technology, analytics, problem-solving talent, or new business models, may actually shift the supply chain trade-off curve. Rather than trading off along a relatively fixed set of points available through traditional actions, the DSC may enable cost savings without any loss in customer satisfaction. Target levels of OTIF quality, at a lower supply chain cost, could be delivered. This isn't just moving along the trade-off curve, this is actually shifting the entire trade-off curve to a more optimal position. Shifting the curve through traditional methods (non-digital) is becoming increasingly difficult as efficiencies have started to reach their maximum.

In theory, everything sounds perfect. Greater performance, enabled through smart technological and process innovations, results in better customer satisfaction with less waste, resources, and cost. Shouldn't all organizations, especially traditional ones, be clamoring for this transformational improvement? What is holding back many organizations from making the necessary changes, investments, and taking immediate action to become more digital?

Many organizations want to change, are willing to change, and plan to change, yet they are either not moving at all, or at best moving very slowly. Change is difficult, and research shows that a majority of large-scale change efforts in organizations fail no matter the complexity (Büyüközkan & Göçer, 2018). Becoming a DSC, especially if your organization is coming from a more traditional operation, is a highly complex endeavor. There are numerous barriers to transforming to a DSC in both management and technology dimensions (CapGemini, 2016). The interconnectedness of the challenge is uniquely daunting. Stakeholders successfully cooperating across organizational boundaries represent a substantial challenge, even for relatively modest business units (Radanliev et al., 2019). The stakes for business transformation are high, yet the barriers to making progress are preventing many organizations from moving forward.

This book is about overcoming these transformational barriers. It is designed to help leaders of organizations seeking to benefit from DSC transformation move the needle. Think of it as a road map, a catalyst, or simply a guidebook of how to get the DSC going in your company.

The key to creating the momentum needed to overcome the complexity of DSC transformation is to break down the effort into discrete performance areas that are more manageable while allowing for the possibility of quick wins, improved organizational support, and the acquisition of needed talent. Attempting a large-scale transformation aggressively may be counterproductive to success as traditional change management methodologies have not been adapted for digital business (Westerman et al., 2014). New approaches are needed to account for the essential ingredients of modern digital business models. A powerful metaphor for this new kind of change is to think of DSC transformation

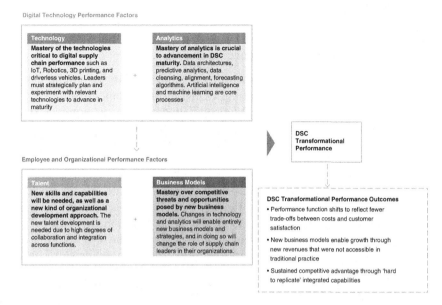

Figure 1.2 The Digital Supply Chain Transformation Framework.

as a mosaic. Supply chain leaders should focus on the "tiles" of performance, technology actions, in analytics, in talent, and segmented business models. By building a strategically selected sequence of performance tiles, and arranging them in the shape of transformation, the odds of success will increase. This book is designed to help create such strategic pathways to change (Figure 1.2).

The DSC Transformation Framework

Transforming supply chains is a complicated business that requires studying multiple layers of customer needs and forecasting, servicing requirements, manufacturing, transportation networks, amongst others. Many decisions regarding how a supply chain will look in a given segment are interdependent and will require integrated actions across functions. Coordinating across functions in large global firms is not something that happens easily or by itself. Looking at the entire picture is too complex for even the best supply chain leaders to develop actions plans for. To help break down the complexity into a framework, decisions must be made about what to include and exclude. Figure 1.2, is a DSC Transformation Framework, a tool to help organize, plan, and develop action plans for the most significant aspects of leading meaningful changes in your own supply chain.

The model is divided into two larger sets of supply chain performance factors from which supply chain leaders can develop plans for.

Digital Technology Performance Factors

The first set of performance factors fall under what we might call "Digital Technology" factors. Being a DSC means taking advantage of core technologies such as Internet of Things (IoT), Robotics, 3-D printing from generative designs, and, eventually, autonomous vehicles. These technologies, when deployed strategically in the appropriate business segments, may yield business performance improvements. Before these improvements are realized, however, we must recognize that digital technologies alone may fall short of providing the intended benefits. To be effective in delivering the desired performance changes, some mastery of data analytics is needed. Of the technologies mentioned, IoT, in particular, will generate enormous volumes of data that will need to be managed well to extract timely and high-quality business insights supporting decisions. Well-designed data architectures, data cleansing, alignment, and ready availability are essential to being able to support more accurate predictive models, forecasts, in addition to machine learning and artificial intelligence processes.

In summary, the digital supply chain must strategically deploy technologies that generate and use analytic data. These core factors have the highest opportunity to produce an outsized impact on supply chain performance.

Employee and Organizational Performance Factors

The DSC Transformation Framework acknowledges that supply chain leaders cannot rely on technology investments alone to meet performance improvement expectations. The second set of key performance factors for supply chain leaders to consider are aligned to employee and organizational issues. Supply chain leaders have recognized that developing digital strategies and deploying technology using data-driven analytics will require access to new skills and capabilities, some of which a firm may not have. Supply chain leaders must develop plans on how to close this talent gap if they are to realize the benefits of the digital supply chain. The right capabilities, deployed in a tailored and, perhaps, newly designed organizational environment are a key part of the performance improvement mix. Just as investments in technology may be blunted or limited by weak efforts in data analytics, so too must digital talent be added to new business models for the digital supply chain to flourish. One of the hallmarks of a mature and high-performance supply chain is its ability to help develop and implement entirely new business models. Business models that utilize a mix of technology and data in ways that respond quickly and creatively to the competitive environment are essential to moving the performance step function for firms.

Transformational Performance Outcomes

This chapter began with a discussion of what digital supply is and the components of a digital supply chain transformation. To close this chapter we now take a look at a proposed list of digital supply chain transformational performance outcomes. Instead of using the term "transformation" broadly, supply chain leaders should be more specific about what their goals are when investing in digital supply chain. The following is a list of outcomes that should be targeted and we propose that they are uniquely attainable by strategic digital actions in the performance areas we have described. This is where the traditional supply chain ends and the digital one takes over. Well-deployed digital actions should enable:

- Performance function shifts to reflect fewer trade-offs between costs and customer satisfaction
- New business models to foster growth through new revenues that were not accessible in traditional practice
- Sustained competitive advantage through "hard-to-replicate" integrated capabilities

Our recommendation is that supply chain leaders keep these performance outcome targets handy as they evaluate digital supply chain investments. If a proposed investment cannot be traced to one or more of these outcomes, it may not meet the threshold of efficacy needed.

Discussion Questions

1. Do you believe a digital strategy will significantly improve your supply chain efficiency and provide a competitive advantage?
2. Is the move to a digital supply chain a new, transformative strategy, or simply the decades-long continuation of the digitization of most business processes?

Chapter One Summary

- Digital transformation is about making a shift from traditional ways of operating, to ones that use data, technology, and business models in innovative ways.

- Digital transformation calls for strong leadership, as it requires more integrated business processes and collaboration.
- Digital transformation is happening globally across most industries. Firms that are slow to react or ignore digital transformation are likely to fall behind their more agile digital competitors.
- The term "Digital Supply Chain" began to gather attention around 2015. It usually refers to the strategic transformation of supply chains, rather than the simple digitization of legacy business processes.
- The benefits of a DSC for firms can be summarized as uniquely reducing the amount of trade-off between costs and customer satisfaction.
- The challenges, complexity, and management demands involved in transforming to a DSC have slowed many firms in their implementation.
- Transformational performance outcomes should foster growth that would be inaccessible in traditional practice and should create sustainable competitive advantage through hard-to-replicate integrated capabilities.
- The key to unlocking this value and advantage is a new, robust, and digitally aware supply chain leadership mindset.

References

AE Consultancy (2015). *What Is Digital Transformation.* http://www. theagileelephant.com/what-is-digital-transformation/. (Accessed 15 October 2016).

Bui, T. (2019). The Digital Supply Chain of the Future: From Drivers to Technologies and Applications. *Proceedings of the 51st Hawaii International Conference on System Sciences (2018).* URI: http://hdl.handle.net/10125/50380. ISBN: 978-0-9981331-1-9.

Büyüközkan, G., & Göçer, F. (2018). Digital Supply Chain: Literature review and a proposed framework for future research. Computers in Industry, 97(5), 157–177.

CapGemini (2016). *Infor, GTNexus, The Current and Future State of Digital Supply Chain Transformation.* http://www.gtnexus.com/resources/papers-and-reports/current-and-future-state-digital-supply-chain-transformation

Michel, R. (May 2017). *The Evolution of the Digital Supply Chain. Logistics Management,* 23–25.

Radanliev, P., De Roure, D. C., Nurse, J. R. C., Montavalo, R. M., & Burnap, P. (2019). Supply Chain Design for the Industrial Internet of Things and the Industry 4.0. Oxford e-Research Centre, Engineering Sciences Department, University of Oxford. 10.20944/preprints201903.0123.v1"

Westerman, G., Bonnet, D., & McAfee, A. (2014). *Leading Digital.* Harvard Business Review Press, Boston, MA.

2 The Customer-Centric Supply Chain

In most executive discussions about supply chain, there is a tendency to begin the conversation broadly, and then narrow it down to the specifics of a particular supply chain element, segment, or piece of data. The idea of the "digital supply chain" is sometimes discussed as if it were a single solution to a large-scale challenge (Saenz & Cottrill, 2019). Experienced supply chain leaders know that there is no single supply chain, but many supply chains, each designed to be optimized across numerous variables. The best supply chain for you and your customers will not only be different from your competitors, it may also differentiate by product segment or geography.

Before we narrow our focus to how the digital supply chain comes into play, let's review a few of the key traits of supply chain excellence (McKinsey & Company & Ghosh, 2008). Excellent supply chains are demand-driven networks that respond with agility to the market. They are also segmented according to customer and market priorities, such as cost, speed of delivery, degrees of customization, quality or precision, and logistics services. For supply chain leaders seeking to capitalize on Digital Supply Chain (DSC) strategies, they will do well to think less broadly about applying digital technologies to their overall supply chains, and instead think about their own supply chain segments. Digital strategies do not mean throwing out basic supply chain principles like segmentation, tailored practices, and end-to-end focus and alignment. They ask themselves, "How can I gain greater insights that will allow me to respond to a given customer market demand?" Understanding customer demand with greater resolution and reduced latency is a strong projected outcome of DSC actions.

The overall goal of supply chain leaders is to effectively meet customer demand for a firm's products and services while managing the costs of sourcing inputs, making products and then delivering them. Traditionally this set of activities, making and delivering, begins with supply chain planning. A good supply chain planner will develop actions plans for different segments based on customer and product demand forecasts. The higher the quality of the forecasts and the more timely they are, the better job supply chain teams can do to deliver on demand plans.

For supply chain leaders, demand forecast accuracy is a mission critical metric that measures how close we are to better-managed inventories and the, at times, conflicting goal of increased customer satisfaction. New analytics techniques show promise in taking the digital supply chain to a new level of performance, including the possibility of real-time demand forecasting (Nguyen, 2017). Reduced information latency, combined with higher predictive power and accuracy, are central to the digital supply transformation.

This chapter will discuss the key developments in data information and analytics that have the most relevance and potential to make an impact on the DSC. Recent advancements in the use of new data architectures, predictive analytics, forecasting techniques, data cleansing, and alignment, are crucial to understanding and developing before you can take advantage of these in a firm's supply chain.

Understanding customer demand deeply and closer to real time should be the mission of a high-performance firm. Accurate and timely predictions of what customers want bring forth a series of economic benefits for the firm and society. On-time, in-full deliveries are just the tip of the data dividend. Reduced waste and energy consumption, greater productivity, reduced inventories, and lower transportation costs (and associated environmental impacts) are just some of the examples a high-performance supply chain can deliver. Understanding customer demand at such deep levels requires timely access to a broader range of on-line data. The strategic objective for the DSC is to "flip" its orientation to the customer side of the value chain (Digital Supply Chain Institute DSCI, 2016). A shift to enhanced customer demand signals unlocks performance improvements that will justify the costs and risks of expanding data sharing across the value chain. Far from merely exploiting consumer data for individual organizational benefit, the digital supply chain will provide worthwhile data dividends that will positively impact our business economics.

The use of Big Data and Analytics in Becoming a DSC

Big Data is a term that is overused and poorly understood. Big data alone, with no accompanying analytics, is unlikely to improve supply chain performance (Sanders, 2014). Big Data Analytics (BDA) will help companies better understand what has happened and help them better predict the future. Huge data sets allow analysts to unearth connections and details formerly hidden. The list of supply chain applications for this approach is quite long and includes: machine failure prediction, black swans, identification of precise purchasing bundles for consumers, causation, inventory placement, and the ability to answer the question "What do our customers want?" With these advances come the additional challenges and implications of how people will react.

Without senior leadership spearheading transformational change, the benefits of these platform investments will go untapped.

A key indicator of BDA supply chain (SC) maturity is the sophisticated use of unstructured data sources in solving SC business performance challenges. Rozados and Tjahjono describe BDA as the process of applying advanced analytics techniques in combination with supply chain management (SCM) theory to datasets whose volume, velocity, or variety require information technology tools from the Big Data technology stack (Rozados & Tjahjono, 2014). They emphasize the need and challenge of leveraging supply chain professionals with the ability to continually sense and respond to SCM-relevant problems by utilizing BDA to provide increasingly accurate and timely business insights (Rozados & Tjahjono, 2014).

Rozados and Tjahjono also found that SCM Big Data sources are commonly generated in unstructured formats difficult to analyze with traditional IT tools (Rozados and Tjahjono, 2014). While data management has focused on expanding velocity and volume capabilities for transactional data, the number of core transactional data sources is relatively small. SCM data sources tend to range between the relatively smaller variations of volume and speed vs. the larger ones in data variety. There is a tendency for the unstructured formats to be high volume/velocity (Rozados & Tjahjono, 2014).

Chen et al. contend "the simple algorithms of big data are more effective than complex algorithms of small data."(Chen, Mao, & Liu, 2014, p 87). This is a key insight. An ability to replace "experts" with faster and more accurate decisions seems possible while reducing subjectivity and increasing speed. The ability to discover previously unknown correlations is emerging. Of particular interest to supply chain leaders is the ability to uncover perceptions and correlations to product demand (Chen et al., 2014).

Chen et al. (2014) discuss a few of the opportunities that BDA could provide to help drive and manage demand:

- ability to monitor and predict low in-stock items in advance
- significantly reduce the impact of late and incomplete shipments
- predict how profitable special quantity deals really are
- forecast the optimal inventory needed for promotions and what the best times to ship the inventory are
- provide retailers with the ability to suggest pricing and allocation strategies where no historical data are available

Finally, in one of the key insights for this chapter, Ittmann notes that "as data and analytics transform organizations, and the landscape within which they operate, it inevitably puts additional new demands on management" (Ittmann, 2015, p 8). "For any organization to achieve what has been outlined in this book it is necessary to take a whole range of steps and actions. These include aspects, such as working across functional areas, data capturing, ensuring data integrity, data management, tools and techniques to perform the necessary analytics analysis, and the human resources capability required to achieve all of this." (Ittmann, 2015, p 8)

The Analytics Maturity Curve

The transformation to a mature stage of using big data and analytics to drive better and faster decision-making in your supply chain is a journey of stages. Think of an analytics maturity curve with the following stages:

1. *Data Identification* – Deciding which elements of structured and unstructured data to acquire and make available in your data store.
2. *Making data available* – Structuring of the data is a traditional next step, cleansing and transforming the raw data sets into a usable format for further analytics processing. This step is changing rapidly with the emergence of "data lake" strategies that are less concerned with the traditional cleansing and alignment of data before processing and are instead focused on the instant availability of raw data, as close to the original source as possible. Advanced analytics tools and processes are making it possible to access and process raw data sets with tremendous speed.
3. *Basic Analytics* – With the accessibility and the rapid ability to cleanse, align and structure raw data from a wide variety of sources, the next step is to begin to apply basic analytics that combine these data sources in new ways to answer questions about supply chain demand closer to real time.
4. *Advanced Analytics, Artificial Intelligence and Machine Learning applications* – with basic analytics productively adding value to supply chain decisions, the next step is to bring in more advanced predictive and forecasting techniques that are becoming available and go behind traditional statistical methods and models.

The data quality and accessibility problem requires interdisciplinary collaboration in order to advance. For instance, information systems experts are needed to provide insight into how data are collected, stored, processed, and retrieved. SCM domain experts are needed to ensure that the problems being studied, the analysis being performed, and results derived thereof are relevant. Additionally, emerging data quality research suggests the need for statistical and analytical experts who are knowledgeable in methods required to measure, monitor, and control data quality. Working together, scholars from these and other disciplines can employ the technologies and techniques to solve the right problems.

To effectively enable returns from BDA and, ultimately, AI/ML investments – data quality is a key challenge and opportunity for SC leaders. Accuracy, timeliness, completeness are critical and certain business questions are better served by a simple algorithm rather than a complex model. The qualities of the analytic models are central to generating useful, accurate and actionable insights.

The Analytics and AI/ML Portfolio Management Strategy

In his book *Demand-Driven Forecasting*, Chase (2013) captures the dilemma facing data savvy supply chain leaders seeking to drive demand.

"Supply processes continue to mature faster than demand. As a result, there is a larger gap to fill in the redefinition of demand forecasting processes to become demand-driven than in any other area of the supply chain. This redefinition of demand forecasting will require new data (downstream point-of-sales [POS] data), processes, analytics, and enabling technologies. To become demand-driven, companies need to identify the right market signals, build demand-sensing capabilities, define demand-shaping processes, and effectively translate demand signals to create a more effective response." (Chase, 2013, p 1)

It is plausible that AI will leapfrog the current traditional supply chain planning function. We reviewed this respected text from 2013, which fails to mention AI at all yet discusses the implications of sensing and demand shaping but without the benefits of the more non-linear AI/ML architectures and models. Supply chain leaders will need to select the methods and architectures that will be most appropriate, based on the type of demand a product is seeking to fulfill. This could influence where AI forecasting models are initially deployed. Perhaps segments that are high value but are at the same time hard to forecast would be prime candidates. A new product launch is one such example.

The Future of Forecasting with Artificial Intelligence

Just as there are traditional forecasting models that are appropriate for specific strategies, companies, industries and products, there is a forecast model selection process that is designed for AI driven forecasts. Business implications include reduced bullwhip effects (BWE), as well as an enhanced ability to shape and influence demand. Fluency needs to be developed in new models – Discrete Wavelet Transform (DWT) and Artificial Neural Network (ANN), for instance, are mentioned in the literature as being a potent combination for outperforming traditional forecasting (Ampazis, 2015; Govindan, 2016; Jaipuria & Mahapatra, 2014). DWT, or Discrete wavelet transforms are discrete, as opposed to continuous, streams of data that show temporal resolution: they capture both frequency and location information (as opposed to Fourier transforms which only capture frequency). Demand data from DWT is fed into an ANN whereby systems learn (progressively improving performance) to do tasks by considering examples, generally without task-specific programming (Ampazis, 2015; Govindan, 2016). The combination of these two technologies constructed in an architecture designed to predict demand has been shown to outperform auto-regressive integrated moving average demand forecasts (ARIMA) (Ampazis, 2015; Govindan, 2016). Even recent comprehensive texts (see Chase, 2013) show ARIMA as the upper-right quadrant of statistical demand modeling.

Another recent study shows a hybrid model where data is first processed by DWT, followed by ANN and adaptive neuro-fuzzy inference system (ANFIS) models (Ampazis, 2015; Govindan, 2016). Studies also conclude that hybrid AI approaches the best ARIMA forecasts when managing BWE. Preprocessing a time series signal with DWT improves AI model performance. ANFIS corresponds to a set of fuzzy IF–THEN rules that have the learning capability to approximate nonlinear functions and is considered to be a universal estimator.

Leadership Issues

This book is not about specific technologies per se, but it is clear that improvements in this set of techniques will need to be closely watched by academics and practitioners alike. Although these types of studies may not be conducted by traditional forecasting practitioners, leadership should work hand in hand with forecasting team leaders on which strategies to build and how to experiment with these new models. The "new" insight is this combination of techniques for SC demand forecasts. Without data lakes and AI pre-processing, forecast data has too much latency and low accuracy, contributing to bullwhip effects and high inventory levels.

Summary

- Transformation to a digital supply chain is often treated by firms as a broad-brush change initiative painted across the entire business, when it might be more effective to address change with greater focus.
- The key attributes of supply chain excellence include: 1.) being networked to respond with agility, 2.) segmented accord to customer needs, 3.) and being more end-to-end.
- Understanding customer demand deeply, accurately, and closer to real time is a high priority essential mission for supply chain leaders.
- The use of both big data and accompanying analytics are needed to

improve supply chain performance. One without the other will blunt the firm's ability to realize gains.

- Big data analytics can provide the capability to monitor and predict stock levels, reduce the impacts of late and incomplete shipping, understand profitability in greater detail, and forecast and manage inventories more effectively.
- Leaders should adopt an analytics maturity approach to managing supply chain data. By identifying, provisioning, analyzing, and then driving to more sophisticated methods, leaders should expect to realize greater rewards for analytics investments.
- The future of demand forecasting with artificial intelligence, as opposed to weighted average approaches, has arrived. Supply chain leaders should begin to invest in these technologies now if they haven't yet started.
- To become a more demand-driven digital supply chain requires leadership that is able to work with data engineers, analytics teams, and forecasters in an integrated manner. Realizing the benefits of digital demand forecasting requires digital leadership to create a vision for the firm and to influence associates, leaders, and partners.

References

Ampazis, N. (2015). Forecasting Demand in Supply Chain Using Machine Learning Algorithms. *International Journal of Artificial Life Research*, 5/1, 68.

Chase, C. (2013). *Demand Driven Forecasting*. Hoboken, NJ: Wiley.

Chen, M., Mao, S., & Liu, Y. (2014). Big Data: A Survey. Mobile Networks and Applications, 19, 171–209. https://doi.org/10.1007/s11036-013-0489-0

Digital Supply Chain Institute (DSCI) (2016). Digital Supply Chains: A Frontside Flip [White paper]. *Center for Global Enterprise*. https://www.dscinstitute. org/assets/documents/a-frontside-flip_white-paper_english-version.pdf

Govindan, K. (2016). *Evolutionary algorithms for supply chain management. Annals of Operations Research*, 242/195. https://doiorg.ezproxy2.library. drexel.edu/10.1007/s10479-016-2227-z

McKinsey & Company, & Ghosh, S. (2008). The Race for Supply Chain Advantage: Six practices that drive supply chain performance [White paper].

Ittmann, H. (2015). The impact of big data and business analytics on supply chain management, *Journal of Transport and Supply Chain Management*, 9(1), 1–9.

Jaipuria, S., & Mahapatra, S. S. (2014). An improved demand forecasting method to reduce bullwhip effect in supply chains. *Expert Systems with Applications*, 41, 2395–2408.

Nguyen, T. (2017). Big data analytics in supply chain management: A state-of-the-art literature review. *Computers and Operations Research*, http://dx.doi. org/10.1016/j.cor.2017.07.004

Rozados, I., & Tjahjono, B. (2014). *Big Data Analytics in Supply Chain Management: Trends and Related Research. Conference Paper, 6th International Conference on Operations and Supply Chain Management.*

Saenz, M. J., & Cottrill, K. (2019). Navigating the road to digital supply chain transformation. *Supply Chain Management Review*, January 2019, 6, 6–7.

Sanders, N. (2014). *Big Data Driven Supply Chain Management*. Upper Saddle River, NJ: Pearson FT Press PTG.

Scoenherr, T., & Speier-Pero, C., (2015). Data Science, Predictive Analytics, and Big Data in Supply Chain Management: Current State and Future Potential. *Journal of Business Logistics*, 36/1, 120–132.

3   Demand Management, Forecasting, and Stimulating Demand

The digital supply chain (DSC) can be a source of demand stimulation to help your organization react rapidly to demand signals, all while keeping cost managed. This chapter focuses on demand as a driver of digital transformation and explores why it is important to generate low latency or real-time data to improve demand forecasting, make better decisions, and create new opportunities that stimulate demand and growth. We will also examine how the evolving DSC strategies can help companies' sense, match, and ultimately drive new demand better.

"Demand Management" refers to how a firm plans, reacts, and ultimately fulfills customer and consumer purchasing of its products and services. A firm that manages demand well does more than fulfill orders on-time and in-full. Key principles must be incorporated to assess how well the firm is managing its demand.

The first aspect is the level of "customer centricity" or customer focus in its demand management (Fader, 2012). Is the firm primarily reacting to customer needs as it drives demand actions, or is it more focused on its own internal activities? A customer-centric supply chain will look deeper into the front end of its transaction processes and react to outside customer behaviors and signals more. A more traditional view of supply chain demand planning is more inside focused and reactive, manufacturing products based on the forecasts and orders it is given rather than on the customers themselves.

A second aspect of good demand management as a supply chain leader involves focusing on revenue growth, rather than simply cost containment and order fulfillment. Supply chain-driven revenue growth can be traced to three main action areas which are:

1. Demand sensing and stimulation – anticipating rather than reacting to demand. Supply chain leaders should seek to accurately anticipate which products are needed, how many of them, the channels they will be sold through, and where product should be stored and

located. Knowledge of customer satisfaction levels for products, packaging, and fulfillment are needed to perform well in this area.

2. Improved demand visibility – gathering and reacting to data about your customers, customer segments, end users, and having, at least, a rudimentary understanding of competitor customer sales activity. How this type of information is obtained will be discussed next. Good demand management requires knowledge and insights that go beyond that which is easily obtained by the supply chain function.

3. Improved ability to satisfy the demand: creating satisfied (or even delighted) customers by reaching them faster, reducing friction in all interactions, and offering them methods of satisfying both of these conditions more innovatively than your competitors (Digital Supply Chain Institute DSCI, 2016).

This list of three action areas is complex to execute effectively. To accomplish each one, the three areas require new sources of data, analysis, access to information, and the ability to process these sources with low latency. Strong supply chain leadership is needed to create conditions for the growth actions.

Leadership Actions Needed for Driving Supply Chain Revenue Growth

Managing the change needed to enable a low latency and high accuracy demand management process incorporates multiple functions and disciplines in most large firms. The design and execution of good demand management processes will require successful interactions both inside and outside of the supply chain function.

Internal Functional Interactions Needed

To create a low latency-high accuracy digital demand management process requires the close collaboration of marketing, sales, and product development functions within the firm. The digital supply chain leader needs to recognize their duties as being more than those of an operations leader. To interact successfully with marketing and sales, for instance, a supply chain leader must establish a new kind of business relationship with these functions. Collaboration and sharing of data and insights, hallmarks of good demand management, can begin in these customer-facing functions. If the supply chain function is simply the recipient of sales, marketing data or plans, it will inhibit the ability of the supply chain leader to enact more digitally integrated, low latency demand management.

External Interactions Needed

Good digital demand management requires the ability to collaborate with customers (such as distributors or retailers), suppliers, and to learn about consumers (if the firm's business model includes them). While the sales function is typically the customer relationship holder for the firm, this does not mean the supply chain function must only rely on sales for critical data and feedback from customers. New technology and digital channels are available too. An e-commerce platform is, at once, a marketing channel, a sales channel, as well as a fulfillment and customer satisfaction channel. As digital business models become more integrated, so must the ways firms operate. Traditional siloed functions may work for non-digital, slower moving customer segments but in a modern digital business model, the walls standing between data and information sharing must be torn down. For firms transforming from older traditional business models to digital ones, the function needed to take the initiative in creating a more collaborative and integrated operational approach may be the supply chain. Again, it is supply chain leadership that will make the difference between an outdated or slow-moving business model, and a more competitive one.

Demand Management – It's All about the Data

In our quest to improve our accuracy and timeliness in making supply chain decisions concerning demand, it is necessary to be more strategic in our use of data. Provost and Fawcett comment in their book *Data Science for Business* "Data, and the capability to extract useful knowledge from data, should be regarded as a key strategic asset" (Provost & Fawcett, 2013, p 9). We agree and also feel that strategic data assets are the underlying key to unlocking digital supply chain performance improvements.

In this section, we discuss the critical aspects of strategic data usage for the supply chain, as well as the leadership implications of moving organizations to higher levels of demand performance.

Before getting into the specifics about the types of data that could be useful to the firm in developing higher quality insights about demand, a general review of the uses of analytic data is in order. By "analytic" data, we mean data that is processed to help managers make better business decisions. Raw data can be useful, but data that is extracted, aligned, and purposefully analyzed using valid analytic models will not only be more useful, but can actually assist managers in making higher quality decisions. First, let's take a look at the different types of analytic data usage.

The most easily obtainable and perhaps most commonly used analytic use of data is causal inference and explanation. Typically, this is the use of historical transaction data to help supply chain demand planners understand what has happened in the past. Historical orders, sales, fulfilment, and inventory levels are some common examples. Analytic tools that help demand planners search, match, fact-find, and aggregate these figures by customer, regions, sales channels, and transportation networks are essential data activities for managing the supply chain. Sales forecasts are often determined from the analysis of this type of analytic business data. Many of these types of analytic techniques have been, and are, common in the more traditional analogue business processes of the past. This type of data is still central to more digital analytic business. To be a truly digital business, however, data analytics need to move to the next level: being predictive.

The Secret to Demand Management Performance Breakthroughs – Predictive Analytics

Explaining what happened in the past is basic management reporting. Being able to accurately predict what will happen in the future goes beyond forecasting and becomes the purview of predictive analytics. Supply chain leaders need to rethink their traditional forecasting and planning methods and include predictive analytic methods in managing demand. As supply chain leaders, you may not have the most up-to-date details on the mechanics of predictive analytics, artificial intelligence, and machine learning, though these techniques form the backbone of digital business and require the right conditions, skills, organizational structures, and data sources to deliver on their possibilities. It is a business imperative to develop a strategic understanding of how these analytic techniques are and could be used in the firm to develop insights and accelerate decision-making.

When used well, predictive analytics, artificial intelligence, and machine learning, collectively called data science, have the power to unlock business insights hidden from view. Data science for business allows business strategists and leaders to explore, discover, optimize, and predict faster and, frequently, better than humans. Ignoring the uses of data science in your business or function represents a lost opportunity to complement and augment the human capabilities of your firm. Employing data science techniques can improve and enhance performance to give you an edge over your competition. Supply chain leaders must create the conditions for data science exploration and solutions to occur. Of course, there are organizational, technological and talent implications when creating this space in your business, but the human aspect is key as decisions involving multiple aspects of the business require courage, influence, and determination. The business benefits of moving from reactive supply chain demand planning to more strategic and predictive planning are central to your firm's digital transformation.

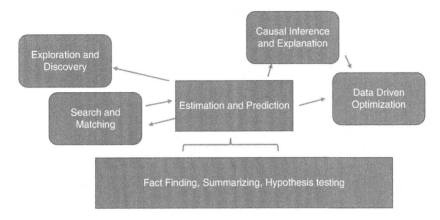

Figure 3.1 Adapted from Foster Provost Conference Presentation (Provost, 2017).

Converting a business into a data science-driven one is the top priority on any Digital transformation leader's agenda.

The conditions of business data science success depend on a number of interrelated factors. Several have been mentioned already, such as organizational design, technology and talent which constitute the data science for the demand planning infrastructure of the firm. Think of these collectively as a metaphorical oil rig and refinery with the oil being the data. Running a data science-driven business requires a high volume of data, better known these days as Big Data.

Data Sources that Drive the Digital Supply Chain

How should the supply chain leader approach data as the strategic asset and input into the digital demand management process? Our work with supply chain leaders reveals a historical tendency to look upon data in a limited way; data must be seen as more than convenient-to-access internal data. Figure 3.2 was created for a recent DSC leadership executive program to help leaders reimagine data sources to be used in supply chain transformation. The chart appears complicated on first sight, but it shows the wide spectrum of data available, from customers (external), to suppliers and network partners, as well as from manufacturing and logistics. These sources illustrate the myriad of connection points across the supply network. Calling this a supply chain is a bit of a misnomer as it is not a true chain of linked, linear, discrete processes and agents. Instead, it is a fluid network of data, information, network partners, customers, consumers, and competitors. Envisioning future data sources requires a basic understanding of how data science for business operates and of the tacit knowledge associated with the deep level of a supply chain business. Consider Figure 3.2.

Data Sources in the Supply Network

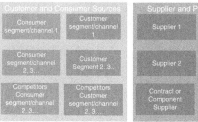

Potential Data Sources:
Internal: ERP, historical sales, marketing campaigns, *External* : Social Media analytics, FB & IG, twitter, influencers, YouTube and television, customer promotions, POS data, market data, economic forecasts, trade policies, weather, sensor data etc.

Potential Data Sources:
Internal: Network partner historical data *External*: channel partner and supplier analytics, forecasts, historical sales, commercially available data (weather's/IBM)

Potential Data Sources:
Internal: constrained capacity planning, sensor-based inventory data, *External*: usage sensors, Control Tower, transportation tracking, customer owned inventories

Figure 3.2 Data Sources in the Supply Network.

Recall the discuss in Chapter 2 where Big Data in supply chain was shown to represent a wide variety of data, including unstructured data such as weather, social media, and IoT sensor data. Figure 3.2 now takes another slice of this idea by stacking the potential data source against network actors/entities. Being able to imagine potential data sources that might improve data science prediction models is one thing. Extracting this information from supply chain network partners is a different matter entirely and falls into the domain of the DSC leader who must develop the skills and techniques needed to unearth useful data essential to a data science business problem. The chart (Figure 3.2) is intentionally complex and serves to inspire creative thinking by supply chain segment designers. To bring this concept to life, we explore a particularly valuable, yet elusive and often unattainable data source for most supply chain demand planners: Point of Sale, or POS, data from retailers.

The Quest for Elusive POS Data

In working with consumer-packaged goods manufacturer supply chain leaders and demand forecasters, one particular data type always seems to come up in discussion. This is Point of Sale data captured by retailers for end user customer sales transactions. Imagine a manufacturer of Sharpie-type markers whose customers, as a large global manufacturer of office products, are distributors, or large retail chains, such as Staples. Distributors and retailers buy these products, then sell them to organizations and individual end users or consumers. As a demand planner for the manufacturing firm, you need to predict, in a timely and accurate way, what customers will be ordering and in which SKUs, regions, and projected volumes. Undoubtedly, important information is shared between your firm and your customers, such as upcoming promotions, changes in demographics, new store openings, and so on. Such information, when correctly and timely utilized, should help improve your demand forecasts. But what about consumer needs and demands? Which color markers will consumers want? What kind of packaging do they prefer? What complementary products do they buy that may indicate additional marker purchases? Are the consumers occasional users of markers, or do they buy them by the basketful? Is there a marker buying season other than back-to-school time? These are the types of insights marketing professionals are particularly interested in. Buying signals, segments, and consumer behaviors are highly prized pieces of information used by firms when innovating with new products, testing new configurations, and satisfying the needs of customers better. While the Marketing function may already be collecting and developing consumer insights, either through direct channels, or through shared retailer information, supply chain leaders may also greatly benefit from the timely analysis of this information. While the logic is there for the sharing of this data, accessing it can be far more difficult.

Why is POS data so hard to obtain?

If you have ever tried to obtain POS data about consumer transactions from distributors or consumers, you know that most trading partners do not share this information freely. While, in theory, it is possible that a trading partner may see some advantage to sharing key marketing and sales objectives, such as for promotional activities, most realize that it is more advantageous to keep valuable consumer data to themselves. Part of the reason is the perceived value of owning the consumer relationship. Distributors and retailers add value to the consumer by making desirable products available to them in a frictionless and pleasant way. Understanding consumer needs, anticipating them, and fulfilling them in ways that create loyalty is the central value proposition for many of these businesses. Consumer loyalty programs that synchronize POS transaction data with individual consumer profiles is especially valued. This type of data, when analyzed and acted upon, potentially enables firms to recognize individual consumer purchasing patterns and allows marketing push actions to drive consumer sales. Marketers with access to this type of data know how valuable it is as it enables more accurate predictions related to consumer purchases, tastes, and projected needs. Firms capable of capturing and harnessing this consumer data can develop algorithmic strategies to anticipate consumer buying and have a distinct source of competitive advantage as well as the potential to build consumer loyalty and higher lifetime value.

What Can Supply Chain Leaders Do to Access POS and Consumer Insights?

Aware of the reluctance of distributors and customers to share key consumer sales data, supply chain leaders can add a few pages to their playbook in the attempt to improve the quality of information they have access to. Firstly, supply chain leaders can develop plans on how to approach and influence their own marketing, sales, and e-commerce functions. Making the case for better information sharing within the firm is a key starting point for making the supply chain more demand agile. Plan on building these relationships strategically by incorporating your own insights and data to establish more valued partnerships. Understanding and being able to demonstrate the downstream impacts of decisions made by front-end functions on supply chain manufacturing and fulfillment is central to this exchange. Leaders should come armed with data and insights that show a command of capacity constraints, inventory levels, and transportation networks. Tie these insights back to external customer performance metrics wherever possible to demonstrate a regard for organizational outcomes, not simply the internal supply chain performance.

Be ready to trade customer focused performance information for both consumer insights developed by marketing analytics teams and customer relationship data from sales teams.

Secondly, it is no secret that digital consumer information captured from on-line or brand-owned direct-to-consumer sales is a treasure trove of data. Every consumer relationship you create, delight, and retain gives your firm higher resolution information about buying behaviors and the raw information to become more predictive. Integrating information across channels is a challenge and can lead to consumer frustration but in an integrated omni-channel business, no consumer will ever walk into a brand-owned retail store-front to find that an on-line direct-to-consumer offer is invalid.

One final, albeit somewhat radical, thought about what supply chain leaders can do to gain access to consumer insights is to learn how to embed consumer feedback data collection into product design and manufacture. Recent advances in technology and the reduced costs of IoT based sensors can trigger the automatic replenishing of products when supply levels fall to predetermined levels in certain segments and industries. This is an example of a digital supply chain-driven business model innovation that increases visibility in consumer needs and allows manufacturers to stay ahead of demand, reduce transactional friction, and potentially increase consumer satisfaction and loyalty.

Digital Data Negotiations Approach

One of the most important aspects of the DSC is a collaboration that extends beyond the boundaries of your organization (Digital Supply

Chain Institute DSCI, 2019). Supply chain leaders know there is a need for more effective collaboration with customers and suppliers in their extended value chains. These needs also encompass shared metrics with customers and suppliers. The most important asset driving these needs is effective and risk-managed sharing of data. The high performing and integrated DSC depend on effective data sharing with our value networks. How can we improve our approach to effective data negotiations with our customer and supplier networks that allows for timely access to key data we need, while not releasing too much of our own valuable data resources in return? To accomplish this trade-off effectively, we need an approach, a methodology based on established negotiating practices and adapted for the rigors of modern data trading. The stakes for negotiating and trading data are high, we should therefore approach it with a solid methodological process that maximizes our access to our partner's data, while protecting and managing access to our own data assets (Digital Supply Chain Institute DSCI, 2019).

Overview

A data negotiations strategy is most valuable when stakeholders are trading across a complex set of issues. It is most important to use this tool to help prepare for trading sessions with partners, as well as negotiating internally to gain bargaining access to your own organization's data assets.

The following process outlines the steps you should take to unlock the value of data sharing with your value chain partners in a thoughtful and risk managed way (Figure 3.3).

The four phases of the process are:

Stage One – Preparing to Negotiate With Data

Preparation is critical to effective data negotiations, just like it is for other types of negotiations. What we are providing is a framework to prepare for data negotiations – a way for you to strategically identify and value the data you need and the value of what you are willing to give in exchange.

One important consideration with data trading and with the DSC, in general, is data governance, data protection, and cybersecurity. Once data is lost or comprised, its market value is diminished or gone. It is critical to incorporate controls for data protection and cybersecurity into how you ultimately structure data trading agreements with your customers and suppliers. The quality of the data you receive is also an important issue. You need to think about how to protect yourself in structuring the data trading agreement. Define the rules and responsibilities for data ownership and regulatory compliance.

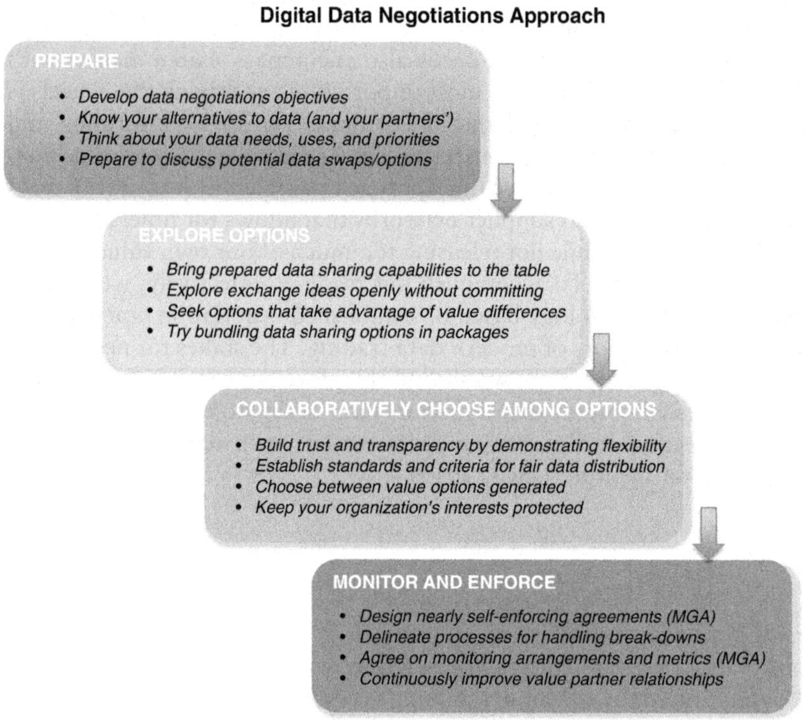

Digital Data Negotiations Approach

PREPARE
- *Develop data negotiations objectives*
- *Know your alternatives to data (and your partners')*
- *Think about your data needs, uses, and priorities*
- *Prepare to discuss potential data swaps/options*

EXPLORE OPTIONS
- *Bring prepared data sharing capabilities to the table*
- *Explore exchange ideas openly without committing*
- *Seek options that take advantage of value differences*
- *Try bundling data sharing options in packages*

COLLABORATIVELY CHOOSE AMONG OPTIONS
- *Build trust and transparency by demonstrating flexibility*
- *Establish standards and criteria for fair data distribution*
- *Choose between value options generated*
- *Keep your organization's interests protected*

MONITOR AND ENFORCE
- *Design nearly self-enforcing agreements (MGA)*
- *Delineate processes for handling break-downs*
- *Agree on monitoring arrangements and metrics (MGA)*
- *Continuously improve value partner relationships*

Figure 3.3 Digital Data Negotiations Approach.

Steps in Stage One: Prepare

Develop data negotiations objectives – Think through the different dimensions outlined in Figure 3.3 to help you prepare for your negotiation sessions with your value chain partners.

Know your alternatives to data (and your partners') – As part of your preparation, develop an understanding of how critical your data needs are, those of your trading partner, and if there are any viable alternatives to them (Digital Supply Chain Institute DSCI, 2019).

Think about your data needs, uses, and priorities – Prioritize your data needs and your trading partners', use assigned values to help quickly spot potential value differences in your data trading sessions. For example, if your partner highly values a data source you possess that is low value to you, this can be used effectively in bargaining for high value data sources held by your partners (Digital Supply Chain Institute DSCI, 2019).

Prepare to discuss potential data swaps/options – Develop an approach for what data you might be willing to trade or share with value partners in exchange for their data you are seeking

Stage Two – Explore Data Negotiations Options

Steps in Stage Two: Explore

Bring prepared data sharing capabilities to the table – Only negotiate data exchanges with your prepared options available. It is easy to make mistakes in the exploration stage without our prepared frameworks at hand.

Explore exchange ideas openly without committing – Utilize the classic mutual gains approach negotiating technique of exploring "what-ifs" with data sources. For example, you might say "If I were able to supply you with advance forecast information, would you be able to supply us with your customer's point of sale data on this category?" Use of inventing without committing allows for value exploration.

Seek options that take advantage of value differences – If you have prepared well, you will have ascribed a numerical value to various pieces of data sources trades. You should look for opportunities to create data trade options that offer low values sources on your side that are high value on your partner's side, and vice versa. By finding, and exploiting these differences, you can create higher value gains for both trading parties.

Try bundling data sharing options in packages – The negotiating strategy of offering bundles of data, rather than negotiating one piece of data time, is well established. Create options that look like this… "If we can offer product launch dates, packaging, and specs on a monthly basis, could you offer us customer historical purchase data in this category, as well as ad response rates for the last 6 months and monthly going forward?" Putting bundles together creates opportunities for advancing mutual value (Movius & Susskind, 2009).

Stage Three – Collaboratively Choose Among Data Negotiations Options

Steps in Stage Three: Collaborate

Build trust and transparency by demonstrating flexibility – In the actual trading sessions with value chain partners, behave in ways that promote trust and transparency. Sure, your partners could try to take advantage of this, and you should always be on the look-out for exploitation of the "negotiator's dilemma", but research has shown that well prepared and initially transparent behaviors, lead to better mutual trading outcomes (Movius & Susskind, 2009).

Establish standards and criteria for fair data distribution – Occasionally you may find a trading partner who is a hard negotiator and is unwilling to back down on a data source or seeks inequitable trades. In these cases, try not to act emotionally and create a downward bargaining spiral, instead, seek to establish what fair trades look like, and refer to them as collaboration intensifies.

Choose between value options generated – Try to choose between the options that have been created in the collaboration sessions, don't pull new options out at the last minute, or allow you partners to do the same, this is where unsustainable, or high risk promises occur, and break trust and long term collaborative partnership value.

Keep your organization's interests protected – A common mistake made in many negotiations is to promise something your organization has not given you permission to trade. Be aware of these limitations, and make sure you don't exceed your authority during heated trading sessions.

Stage Four – Monitor and Enforce Data Negotiations Agreements

Steps in Stage Four: Monitor and Enforce Agreements

Design nearly self-enforcing agreements (Movius & Susskind, 2009) – Remember that it's important to create data trading agreements that have a low cost to sustain and are easy to audit.

Delineate processes for handling breakdowns – Breakdowns in data sharing are likely in some cases, prepare for them ahead of time and discuss how they will be handled. This is much better than attempting to go back after a deal has been made and seek remedies without a defined process.

Agree on monitoring arrangements and metrics (Movius & Susskind, 2009) – Establish how data sharing will occur, be monitored and measured up front. Do not agree to costly and unauditable arrangements. Timeliness of data is a currency at times, if the agreement is for monthly customer data, getting it 6 months from now reduces its value substantially. Agree on frequency of feeds, as well as latency up front.

Continuously improve value partner relationships (Movius & Susskind, 2009) – This is the key to unlock shared and integrated value in data sharing agreements.

Taking the Next Steps – What Actions Can Leaders Take Now?

To conclude this chapter, we introduce a framework to assist in the process of planning transformational actions to become a more digital demand managed and analytical supply chain. Additionally, we share a set of discovery questions to guide strategic discussions and, ultimately, actions within your teams.

In the figure below, a Digital Supply Chain Analytics Maturity Model is shown to help leaders assess and plan for strategic improvement actions. Confronting the difficult task of running operations efficiently and finding ways to improve performance can be a frustrating task for supply chain leaders as they focus on future transformation plans: transforming into a true digital company does not happen overnight. This chapter presents a three-horizon model inspired by the venerable McKinsey model first developed by Baghai, Coley and White (Baghai, Coley, & White, 2000). Imagine horizon one as the current landscape and environment where smooth operations are maintained. Just beyond this horizon is the "growth" horizon, which should be accomplished in perhaps 9–18 months from now. Actions taken in the growth horizon enable the capture of revenues or reduced costs not currently in our grasp. Beyond this lies horizon three, reachable within a few years of current operations, and it represents the "transformation" horizon. It is aspirational, yet within reach if the actions in horizon one and two can be brought to fruition (Figure 3.4).

Leadership Actions to Drive Digital Transformation

In the near-term operational horizon for analytics capability, leaders should begin by developing a clear sense of current capabilities, as well as by establishing high-value operational goals for business segments. Having interviewed numerous supply chain and operations leaders for

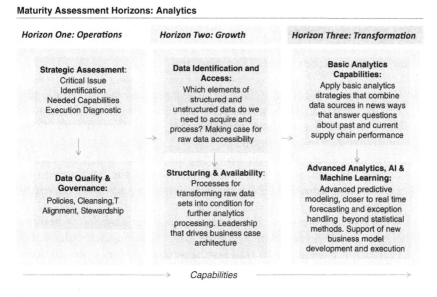

Figure 3.4 Maturity Horizon Map: Analytics.

many years, we know the universal starting point for building analytic capability is improving data quality and governance. Access to high quality raw data ranks amongst the most important aspects of digital transformation and represents a key building block enabling the implementation of more sophisticated analytic techniques. Though clearly a technical subject, in particular the cleansing and alignment of data sets from disparate sources, the key determinant of success is leadership in establishing data governance as a business priority and making governance an integral part of management practice.

In the growth horizon, leaders begin to identify specific sources of data to enable digital business models and segment performance improvements. Leadership is required to narrow the scope of data to the strategic elements most needed to unlock performance efforts. Once the elements or sources are identified, it may be no simple matter accessing them and, subsequently, providing access to the analytic users. As in our POS data example above (and in many other cases), leadership knowledge in data trading, negotiation, and influence is required to create access to transformational sources of information.

The final step in this model is the high-performance usage of data to drive business model innovations and create transformational business improvements. Building the technical capabilities, finding the right talent, and creating the right organizational structures to enable data analytic exploration, not simply exploitation, is the ultimate goal.

A Set of Demand Data Action Steps – A Leader's Guide

While digital transformation is our ultimate goal, it is helpful to have a short, manageable set of steps that focus attention on demand data to efficiently improve operations. The steps are:

1. *Determine a high-value business segment*: instead of randomly seeking demand data actions across an enterprise, focus instead on high margin, high-value segments that can most benefit from improved demand management.
2. *Determine which data can help*: use the models and tools in this chapter, as well as the discussion questions in the next section to narrow data sources to those that are existing, and/or are currently inaccessible.
3. With potential strategic data sources identified, *develop a plan to acquire it*. Identifying data is not the same as having accessible data. Leadership is required to trade or negotiate, influence and bargain your way to acquire as many strategic sources as are feasible. Not all useful data sources may be accessible.

4. For data sources you can acquire or access, a *plan for how to use it* is needed. Big data sets, while exciting to have access to, will not automatically provide useful or accurate insights. Determining how to transform, align, and build analytic models that will yield reliable results must follow.

5. *Determine business actions*: brilliant data scientists, analytics experts, complex data lakes, algorithms, and models ultimately require leaders to take action on insights. Knowing how to react to the findings of the digital information is essentially a leadership and management capability.

Leadership Tools – Guiding Questions for You and Your Teams

In our work with supply chain leaders in companies around the world, it has become clear to us that there is no "cookbook" or set of prescribed actions that are universal for all businesses seeking to become digitally advantaged. Instead of check lists of actions to perform or consider, we have concluded that a set of management questions to ask yourself and your teams in a guided fashion is more useful. These questions have been posed to help guide executive education participants through the complex thought processes of leading digital businesses. They are presented here as a set of resources to consider as we close this chapter on demand management.

Driving Questions – Demand Management

- Can you identify and access new sources of real-time data that could improve your company's ability to sense demand? What are they?
- What can you do to enable your own company's supply chain function to take on a greater role in stimulating and shaping demand?
- What can your organization do to improve its level of supply chain lower latency or real-time responsiveness?
- What does your team recommend the organization do that is practical and implementable within 2 months?
- How does your plan deepen or extend the company's relationship with its customers? What are the data sources that will help the company to either better sense, manage, match, or stimulate demand?
- How will you access the data you will need to become more demand focused? Are there other functional areas or stakeholders you will need to involve?
- How will you allocate resources and prioritize improvements?
- What are the leadership implications of making these ideas happen?

Case Example

Global Manufacturer and Brand Marketer
of Consumer-packaged Goods

Industry and Competitive Landscape

The consumer personal care products business is characterized by the dominating presence of a handful of key global players at the top the industry, as well as number of growing segments of newer, independent brands focused on a narrower range of products. Our case company is at the top of the industry and has developed a reputation as being one of the top supply chains in the world. How does one of the world's biggest, and best supply chains adapt and evolve? What are the key strategic business actions they are taking to remain competitive, innovate, and deliver on the complexity of having thousands of SKUs, size, flavor, configurations for each of its hundreds of categories, manufactured and delivered to over eighty countries around the world? The market leader of this set of high volume, modest margin core business must have something we can learn from about designing high performance supply chains, and how digital segment strategies can help us get there.

Organizational Situation

In spite of the emphasis in this volume on what we have defined as digital supply chain, many of the key strategies the world's best supply chains develop are still trying to solve the same evergreen problems supply chain leaders have been struggling with for decades. In this case, the challenge is how to improve the overall firm's ability to better forecast demand, management inventories, and improve visibly of products in the supply chain pipeline. Bullwhip effect, created by information latency is still the core issue to solve, even for one of the worlds' top supply chains. This and other key organizational strategic initiatives should sound familiar to business leaders from all ranks and functions. Among the initiatives we see:

- Increased focus on innovation – being a consumer products business with increasing competition from store brand label and independent brands this is now and will continue to be essential.
- The need to become more agile – speed and the ability to change direction in products, networks, and consumer preferences quickly is also the new normal. Also the focus on balancing responsiveness with cost of capital and service levels.
- An ability to deliver true End-to-End (from consumer demand to supplier response) planning and execution is also a key part of supply chain strategies of firms around the world

- Leveraging analytics to make better decisions – at the crux of the digital transformation firms are undergoing, and
- Being more data and systems driven – relying less on individual judgments and instead utilizing data and real-time information to make faster, better decisions

The supply chain leadership response must include digital actions in order to realize the objectives of these strategic performance initiatives.

Leadership Response

To enable the activation of these strategies, the case firm created working teams aligned to critical business operations. Some teams are:

- End-to-End Initiative team which focused on service levels and inventory, seeking savings opportunities while reducing trade-offs
- Data analytics team which developed the right competencies to drive faster and more data driven decision making
- Leadership and Change team which focused on the mindset change, helping associates move away from historically asset utilization driven decisions, that is simply "how much produce", and behave based on more synchronized supply and demand

Digital Supply Chain Implications – Actions

To illustrate the complexity and integration of the global supply chain function that was envision, the following chart shows the different working levels and some of the associated technology supporting them. The case company invested millions of dollars in technologies, pilot programs, process redesign, and systems integration. The chart should give some indication of how sophisticated the workflows of a global integrated supply chain look like (Figure 3.5).

Digital Supply Chain Readiness

On looking at Figure 3.5, the question might be, where does the DSC begin, and where does it end? Or is digital just the new way of doing supply chain business? While there are no specific technologies listed in the chart, imagine modules from firms like, SAP are adapted, developed, and support several of the work functions. Imagine leading a supply chain if this scope and magnitude without some degree of integration. Here are some of the key elements of the integrated model:

Demand Sensing: Timely knowledge of customer sales and analytics. Sales Inventory & Operations Planning (SI&OP) consensus used as

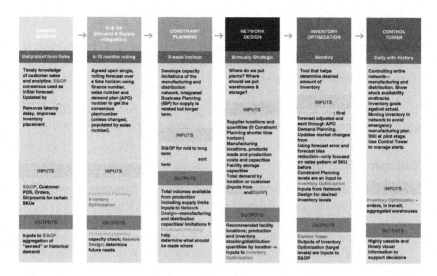

Figure 3.5 An Integrated Demand Management Model.

initial forecast. Updated by Demand Sensing. Removes latency delay. Improves inventory placement.

SI&OP: Agreed upon single, rolling forecast over a time horizon using finance number, sales number, and demand plan (APO) number to get the consensus plan/number (unless changed, populated by sales number).

Constraint Planning: Develops capacity limitations of the manufacturing and distribution network. Integrated Business Planning (IBP) for supply is related but longer term.

Network Design: Where do we put plants? Where should we put warehouses & storage?

Inventory Optimization: Tool that helps determine desired amount of inventory

Control Tower: Controlling entire network—manufacturing and distribution. Show stock availability and tracks inventory goals against actual. Moving inventory in network to avoid emergency manufacturing plan. Control Tower is used to manage alerts.

Control tower is an up to the minute example of where the DSC is going. Control is a tool that is by very definition is dependent on the successful implementation of a more digital and integrated supply chain function. It receives the inputs of the Inventory Optimization module, which tracks orders, in transit goods, and inventories in aggregated warehouses. To operate effectively, Control Tower requires a lot of timely processed information from all around the customer distribution region under consideration. If control tower is working well, it is providing real time, or close to real time, aggregated information about where inventories are located and where they are going to be. As a supply chain manager faced with a decision about whether to send out of stock items to a customer using expedited freight, a costly decision, I need to know the answers to questions like, "is this inventory anywhere else nearby", and "how profitable and critical is this customer, do I incur a shipping cost margin hit on its behalf, or not?" Without timely integrated information as the control tower might provide, I may need to make supply chain decisions with less than high quality information. At the time of this writing, during the COVID-19 pandemic, firms that have been slowing moving to develop the complex and sophisticated systems required to enable control tower, have started to say they will actually do it.

The final point to make in this case before we ask some questions overall is "how to we enable our supply chain associates to trust the data our sophisticated systems are producing?" The case firm invested years and millions of dollars into developing a more integrated digital end-to-end supply chain. In the end, many benefits of this investment rely on the behaviors and actions of supply chain associates. In a firm with a long history, and associates with many years of experience, there is likely some challenge in getting them to trust the data outputs generated by the new demand planning systems. If I'm a plant manager who has been prioritizing manufacturing runs based on relationships I have built over many years with regional sales managers. How easy will it be for me to now make decisions based on the recommendations of the demand planning algorithms? Will I immediately trust this data over what my regional contacts are asking for?

Digital Supply Chain Case Questions

1. How did the case company obtain the support, both operational and financial, to undertake such a large-scale integrated supply chain initiative?
2. Is this case example a true example of the digital supply chain we have defined it in this book? Or is it more traditional?
3. What are some examples of competitive threats that the case firm should be aware of? What kinds of digital supply chain strategies might they be competing with?
4. Is the case presenting challenges that are technology focused, or more about organizational behavior?
5. How could the case company ensure that there is support and compliance from its associates as they begin to transition over to utilizing data and information generated by the end-to-end systems and algorithms?
6. How much support do you think this firm's supply chain leadership will need in order to accomplish its stated goals and experience performance improvements?

7. Does this case firm's strategy also account for developing innovative products that will delight customers, increase satisfaction, and increase revenues?

Summary

- The DSC represents a shift away from an order fulfillment orientation, to one that is more focused on demand stimulation while managing costs.
- Demand management addresses how firms plan, react, and fulfill customer and consumer orders of its products and services.
- A Customer-Centric supply chain looks more deeply into the front-end of transaction processes and reacts faster to customer behaviors and signals coming from outside the firm.
- To realize the goals of demand sensing, stimulation, improved visibility, and satisfaction requires new sources of low latency data and more integrated analytics capability.
- Supply chain leaders need to collaborate more closely and effectively with marketing, sales, and product development within firms in order to realize DSC benefits.
- Supply chain leaders also need to develop greater capacities to collaborate with, learn about, and share information with customers and partners.
- Supply chain leaders should enable the development of more predictive forecasting, going beyond traditional planning.
- Supply chain leaders seeking new sources of information in the quest for better forecasting should practice digital data negotiations techniques, which utilize classic techniques of negotiations and apply them to the acquisition and trading of data with internal and value chain partners.
- A set of demand data actions that will focus attention and efficiently improve operations involves; 1) determining high-value segments, 2) determining which data will help execute the segment design, 3) developing a plan to acquire the data, and 4) planning actions on how to use the insights and results.

References

Baghai, M., Coley, S., & White, D. (2000). *The Alchemy of Growth: Practical Insights for Building the Enduring Enterprise*. Cambridge, MA: Basic Books.

Digital Supply Chain Institute (DSCI) (2016). Digital Supply Chains: A Frontside Flip [White paper]. *Center for Global Enterprise*. https://www.dscinstitute. org/assets/documents/a-frontside-flip_white-paper_english-version.pdf

Digital Supply Chain Institute (DSCI). (2019). Data Trading as a Catalyst for Digital Supply Chain Transformation [White paper]. *Center for Global Enterprise*.

https://www.dscinstitute.org/assets/documents/2019DSCI_CatalystProgram_whitepaper_FINAL.pdf

Fader, P. (2012). *Customer Centricity: Focus on the Right Customer for Strategic Advantage*. Philadelphia, PA: Wharton Digital Press.

Movius, H., & Susskind, L. (2009). *Built to Win: Creating a World-Class Negotiating Organization*. Boston, MA: Harvard Business Press.

Provost, F. (2017, February 17). *Big Data [Conference Presentation]. CorpU Supply Chain Executive Council*, Sebastopol, CA, United States: O'Reilly Media.

Provost, F., & Fawcett, T. (2013). *Data Science for Business*. Sebastopol, CA, United States: O'Reilly Media.

4 Leading a Demand-Driven Supply Chain

Becoming a more demand-driven supply chain takes vision, persistence, influence, and a willingness to stick to the hard work of pursuing change for this process is a complex agenda filled with choices. Creating a digital supply chain (DSC) transformation agenda should take into consideration multiple facets of the journey you are about to undertake, a journey that requires clear leadership if the digital transformation is to happen.

Chapter 3 described the factors supply chain leaders must account for to determine where energy and effort must be placed as your firm will be making decisions regarding data sources, customers and consumers, and how to cooperate with internal and external partners. Traditional firms seeking to become more digital face an even larger set of issues and choices, as their existing business models, technology and processes will need to change before transformation benefits can be realized.

In terms of designing and building high performance supply chains, Soumen Ghosh, a well-known professor of supply chain at Georgia Tech's Scheller School of Business, made a convincing case when speaking to an audience of senior supply chain executives. Ghosh opened his executive education presentation with the seemingly simple question: "What is a good/excellent supply chain for you?" (Ghosh, 2011). This question makes executives consider the fundamentals of their supply chains and how to define what "good" and "excellent" mean. Ghosh asks executives to think less about the idea of supply chain as a broad function, and more of individual business segments because the best supply chain is a segmented supply chain, one that is tailored to the specific characteristics of your customers and how to satisfy them (Ghosh, 2011). When looking for answers on how to approach the digital transformation of a supply chain, do not paint organizations with a broad digital brush, instead begin by looking at customer segments to determine which supply chain design would best meet or exceed their demands. Digital supply chain is not a one-size-fits-all approach. It must be tailored to segments, but designing these segments is a nonlinear process. And so the journey begins.

Where Do I Start the Digital Journey?

Working with traditional firms at the early stages of digital transformation, one common error typically arises: Investing in specific technologies at scale. To initiate discussions on the digital transformation by even considering technologies at scale is a mistake. Do not rush into investing in IoT sensor technology or 3D printing as a solution for manufacturing. Take the time to study and test these promising new technologies and how they can be applied to the supply chain by establishing a laboratory for technology innovation on a smaller scale. Become familiar with how technology applications can fuel product design, manufacturing, or distribution improvements, but be careful about becoming heavily technology driven. The selection, development, and deployment of technology to a business should be done in concert with the customer segment design. Technology is not the be-all and end-all of a DSC transformation. Rather, it is part of the solution to meeting customer needs better, reducing the cost of meeting those needs, and capturing new market growth. Technology is a key part of the equation, but it rarely translates into a reliable starting point for digital transformation.

We will revisit the question around technology selection in Chapter 6. It cannot be discounted that technology is a great source of competitive advantage and does play a central role in enabling digital business. Consider the difference between a segment strategy that is developed and based on technology as its core decision frame, versus one that is developed based on customer demand insights. There is an advantage to building a transformation model, or pathway, that has a basic order of operations. It may not be a linear progression, but the benefits gained in improving performance by thinking about talent implications, technology issues, and risk management considerations in specific response to a particular customer segment supply chain design are compelling.

The DSC Leadership Road Map

In response to the evergreen question of "How and where do I start the digital transformation process?", we have developed a leadership "road map" to help guide you through numerous interrelated decisions. The road map is not a check list or prescription. It is a simple way or orienting DSC strategies that places the emphasis on the customer side of the business. Having a map also allows supply chain leaders to coordinate efforts across functions and departments.

Let's review Figure 4.1 to begin understanding the road map concept.

Before delving into the overall road map components, review the DSC Transformational Performance goals presented in Chapter 1. Think of the goals as the "destination" on the map, a point fixed on the horizon

Digital Supply Chain Leadership Road Map

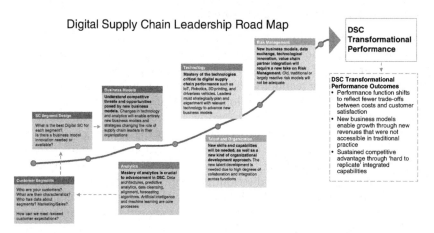

Figure 4.1 The Digital Supply Chain Leadership Road Map.

that we are aiming for in our digital transformation efforts. Leadership will benefit from clearly defining what these goals are for your organization and from having a strategic alignment around the goals, terminology, and metrics measuring success.

DSC Transformational Performance Goals

As was discussed in Chapter 1, successful firms must clearly define what they mean by digital transformation. If the supply chain sourcing function views digital transformation as automating supplier scorecards and manufacturing views it as using 3D printing while logistics views it as using IoT sensors to keep tabs on in transit inventory, then the supply chain leader will find it difficult to rally the firm around more integrated end-to-end goals. In our work with supply chain leaders, we have found it useful to clearly define digital transformation goals in terms of performance improvements, rather than technology deployment. The goals are:

- Fewer trade-offs between Costs and Customer Satisfaction
- New business models that enable revenue growth inaccessible for traditional practices
- Sustained competitive advantage gained through implementing "hard to replicate" integrated capabilities

These goals give supply chain leaders measuring sticks with which they can evaluate DSC segment designs. If a segment design does not deliver at least one of the targeted goals as a result, then that design should be reconsidered. As segment design actions and decisions are taken, these goals should always be evaluated to protect you from drifting away from them. The design actions can also be viewed as design constraints or principles, offering guardrails to decision-making.

With these goals in mind, let's review the roadmap waypoints.

Step One – Who Are Your Customers?

Who are your customers? – What are their characteristics? – How can we meet/exceed customer expectations?

When meeting marketing professionals a renowned Wharton marketing professor who is considered a go-to thought leader for many global CMOs, has one simple question: "Who are your customers?" Being on the receiving end of this question may seem childish. "Of course, I know who my customers are" one might say. But then, after a somewhat uncomfortable moment or two, some sheepishly admit they may not have a finely tuned understanding of what is a central starting point for businesses. While marketers should have a good grasp of customer segments, it may not be the first thing to come to mind for supply chain leaders. Upon being handed a forecast or when called on to execute a manufacturing plan, supply chain leaders could overlook the notion of customer needs driving supply chain decisions. For DSC transformation, understanding your firm's customer, consumer characteristics, demands, needs, and preferences by segment is the key to unlocking transformational performance. When interacting with your firm's marketing team as you seek a better understanding of demand signals, be sure to zero in on specific customer segment characteristics. Do certain segments value quality or price? Speed and convenience or low cost? Individualized experiences or anonymity? Control over reordering safety stock or automatic replenishment? Undoubtedly, there is a long list of characteristics you should try to identify for your most critical current and prospective customers. The characteristics you uncover in your customer segments should be front and center as you design supply chains to meet or exceed their needs and expectations. A supply chain that is designed for low cost, for example, may frustrate a higher value segment customer that is counting the days until an order arrives. Customers who desire certain packaging and shipping requirements and are not configured to receive orders that are off-spec may become a flight risk if their needs continue to be unmet. These segments must be developed carefully and understood deeply for there are many other examples such as the ones above. If you are missing key insights about the segment, find a way to uncover them. Seeking data and information from internal as well as external sources is key. While you are at it, you can seek insights about your competitors' segments that could very well be a critical source of information to help you design your own supply chains. As we will discuss in the next section, there are insights about segments which may not reside in the data available to us. Before fully designing a supply chain for a segment, you will need to find insights hidden from apparent view.

Step Two – Using Analytics to Uncover Segment Opportunities

What are The "Non-intuitive" Insights We Can Develop About Our Customers and Consumers?

The sophisticated use of analytics has become the hallmark of the high-performance digital enterprise and digital native companies have built their businesses around (Lund et al., 2013). Algorithms, platforms, and customer recommendation engines fuelled by real-time clicks are what we think of when we imagine a modern digital business whereby demand is often driven by machines rather than people. The recommendation engine is a clear example. Individual customer product recommendations generated by algorithms and data produce a high percentage of follow-on revenue increases. The specific recommendations generated may not always be completely intuitive, yet they often uncover a sales opportunity hidden from view. Similarly, marketing professionals and product innovators may use data analytics to discover nonintuitive insights about customers and consumers. For example, the buyer of a pair of signature athletic shoes may not be a young teenager, but a middle-aged mother. The tools and techniques of the marketer have focused on finding these prized business insights for many years. How often are such insights used by supply chain leaders to develop their segment designs?

The skill sets required to go beyond what is apparent in segment data can be daunting as we enter the realm of data architecture, data cleansing, alignment, predictive analytics, and forecasting algorithms. Artificial intelligence and machine learning are core processes used to drive e-commerce sales on company-owned websites, as well as social media platforms (Xu, 2014). What happens on retailor and distributor websites is much fuzzier for many firms. The point is that analytic muscle can be flexed in designing supply chain segments, as well as in more operational demand forecasts and fulfillment networks. Supply chain leaders can and should be involved in decisioning based on upstream business insights just as the more predominantly customer-facing functions of the firm are. If you lack access to this set of resources, the leadership move is to negotiate, trade, and influence your way into them. Leaving the data analytic value on the table is not a viable business option in the face of digital competition.

Armed with knowledge and insights about the key, most profitable and critical segments, and those we are targeting for growth, leaders are prepared to design their new digital supply chain segments.

Step Three – Designing the New Digital Supply Chain Segment

What Is The Best Digital Supply Chain for Each Segment? – Is There A Business Model Innovation Needed or Possible?

Given a particular segmented set of customer and consumer needs, preferences, and expectations, we are now set to design a DSC for them. What choices make up a DSC segment design? The list will be unique for the particular industry and customer segment to be developed but ideas for discussion include:

- Channel preferences – online, bricks and mortar, distributor, specialty retailer, big box retailer, volume and replenishment schedules, inventory monitoring methods, inventory holding preferences, warehousing, and transportation network services.
- Product preferences – product packaging, service and support needs, customization levels, follow-on product extensions, substitutes, warranty and repair processes, product design choices, product quality, interoperability with 3rd party products
- Brand preferences – exclusivity and availability, channel decisions (high-end retail vs. big box), inventory holding levels (safety stock levels), marketing, and promotional strategies

This list is not exclusive but demonstrates what your team should consider as they develop segment designs. While we have been advocating the idea that supply chain designs are unique to customer segments, it does not exclude the sharing or reusing of technologies or processes across segments if there are opportunities for efficiencies. Be aware that design decisions cannot be made based on efficiency alone; they must be made on the basis of the customer segment impact upon them. While the idea of holding inventories, and the costs of doing so, may seem antithetical to driving down supply chain cost, the customer impacts of a stock-out may be significantly higher in the long run. Stock-out costs are not just limited to a single lost sale but may create opportunities for customers to consider substitutes and loss of future revenues.

DSC Segment Design Example

For this exercise we imagine a customer segment in a consumer-packaged goods business who is a manufacturer of consumer cleaning and personal hygiene products and whose customer is a national retail pharmacy chain. The retail pharmacy business is high volume, low margin, and is extremely competitive across brands and retailers. Retailer shelf space is limited as are inventory storerooms. Distribution hubs are located regionally and within a one-day reach of our ground transportation distribution network. The segment in question is oral hygiene products. If we review the segment prompts above, we can develop a snapshot of the segment profile.

- *Channel Preferences*: This segment is bricks and mortar retail through distribution centers to individual retail locations without storage capacity on site. We have good visibility into future orders and replenishment schedules at the distribution center level. We do not currently have any way of monitoring inventory levels in our customer's distribution warehouses. We do not have visibility into transportation schedules or networks at a retail store level. There is little or no e-commerce presence or sales.
- *Product Preferences*: Distribution centers for the customer prefer to process cases of our products that conform to weekly shelf capacities. They do not want to deliver and store multiple cases of product to retail locations which do not have the space or staff to manage inventories. Cases should contain products ready to be placed on shelves with minimal reconfiguration or unpacking. Support for products should be available to pharmacists where there are medicinal values, and directly for consumers for after-sales support. Currently, there are few opportunities for product customization. All of our products have reasonable substitutes within our own brand for each category. Product quality is targeted towards a value, or moderate cost consumer. Our products are easily substituted with our competitors' brands and in some cases, the white label store brands.
- *Brand preferences*: We do not have any exclusive customer products currently. Our customer's retail experience is about convenience and health. Empty shelves create a negative impression on their consumers. Large quantities of inventory are not made visible to consumers (as opposed to big box retail). Our customer's marketing function is highly centralized and creates regional promotions.

DSC Segment Initial Design

Using this example, it becomes obvious that one supply chain will not meet the needs of this customer. A supply chain designed for a big box retailor, or a large-scale e-commerce retailor, would not look like the design for this national retail pharmacy chain. The digital segment design for our sample company needs to have an extremely high degree of timely forecast accuracy. Stock outs must be avoided. Case packaging should be tailored to weekly shelf stock sizing. Knowledge of promotions at a retail level are highly important to adjust order sizing to temporary increases in demand. Packaging should be designed to make in-brand product substitutes easy for consumers. Health and safety branding should align with the customer's retail brand attributes.

DSC Opportunities

What does this mean for our DSC design? Ideas will emerge as we develop the segment strategy, such as offering support for the development of e-commerce direct-to-consumer sales in partnership with the retail brand. Developing a DSC strategy aligned to marketing for this type of business model shift could deepen the business relationship with this customer. Developing consumer insights that help the brand differentiate itself for the customer is another possibility. Consumer data knowledge owned by our manufacturing and distribution networks could be useful in trading for retail point of sale (POS) data. Better POS data could help in managing inventories on behalf of the customer. Better visibility into regional finished goods inventory levels, as well as stock in transit, will also help manage inventories for this customer which may end up being the number one segment attribute we should design for.

Step Four – Business Model Review Cycle

Before we finalize our DSC segment design, a review of the attributes of the segment and testing for possible changes to our business models is in order. A competitive review to gather intelligence on what other firms are doing to address the segment under evaluation should also be included. By framing our evaluation by segment, and then designing the supply chain according to insights about the segment needs including possibilities revealed by new technologies, we should be open to new ways of delivering value to the targeted customers. A shift to a more direct-to-consumer business model enabled by e-commerce is a dramatic example whereby the supply chain function could play an integral role in a segment business model shift of this magnitude. To a lesser degree, a supply chain segment strategy more open to direct customer service support after market is a contemporary example. Initially, Amazon may be a retail channel for my customer, but customers could be captured using a new business model for after-sales support and follow-on sales with the right integration of services.

Sensor-based technologies, customer loyalty data and programs, social media interactions post-sale, such as product posts comments, are examples of new forms of digital information which allow a new business model opportunity to have the potential to be transformational. The key for this leadership roadmap process is to ensure, as you redesign the segment for DSC, that you do not simply automate the old processes using new technologies (Bugihn et al., 2017). It is crucial to look for ways to increase segment value by improving customer satisfaction, increasing revenues, and improving efficiencies. We suggest iterating this loop of customer segment, analytic insights, segment design, and business model several times before proceeding to the stages of implementing a new DSC segment process. From a leadership perspective, to effectively iterate in this way the necessary level of integration with the broader firm requires a new way of working compared to traditional business models. The DSC leader will need to be comfortable transcending functional barriers in the firm in order to effectively participate in the business modeling process. The digital redesign of business models will require the integrated support of senior leadership across several functions to be effective.

Step Five – What Talent, Skills and Capabilities Do I Need to Execute This Design?

Having conceived of the design of a DSC segment, and perhaps having some aspects of a new or modified business model on the table, you need to tap into the requisite organizational and network partner talent to bring the segment design to life. In our next chapter, we go into greater detail on the talent management strategies required to be successful in a more DSC world. For the purposes of this leadership road map, the key point is to wait until your segments are designed before beginning the process of determining which digital skills are required to execute them. This may be too slow, too expensive, or impossible as highly skilled digital talent is scarce and difficult to attract and acquire. With the segment designed, you will need to assign or influence talent from the right parts of the organization to develop and deploy them. As will be discussed in the next chapter, leaders may need to deploy new organizational designs, as well as influence other functions, in order to effectively execute the new segment actions. Digital segment designs are often more integrated in how they operate where new demands on both internal talent and new relationships with external value chain partners can be created.

Step Six – Which Technologies Are Available to Execute This Design?

We finally come to the technology selection moment in our digital leadership journey! You may be thinking that this is too late in the game for the technology discussion. In fact, technology is part and parcel of the entire segment design process as it is integral to the discovery of insights used to understand customer needs and is part of the business modeling process in imagining new ways to satisfy customer demand (Wu et al., 2016). This point of the digital journey is not the first time we have thought about how to use technology. It is, however, good practice to delay the selection of technologies until the segment has been defined and designed. Making technology selection a key part of the design process runs the risk of the segment process being made to fit the technology, rather than the technology fitting the segment. The design process is iterative and needs insights about technology capabilities to take advantage of them. Leadership and discipline is required to delay the investment in scaled technologies until their best use has been determined. There is also the chance you may overinvest in a technology that might be useful in a less-than-critical customer segment. Your highest and best investments in technology should be dedicated to areas where your segment values are highest, or where a strategic implementation of technology could become a source of competitive advantage (Alaybayi et al., 2019). As mentioned earlier, one of the goals of becoming digital is to create "hard to replicate" supply chain value. This is where strategic technology deployment can mean the difference between automating an existing process and creating a new transformational business outcome.

Step Seven – What New Business Risks Might This Design Create?

In our final waypoint along our digital leadership journey we come to risk management.

New business models, new data exchanges, technological innovation, and value chain partner integration require a new take on risk management. Existing or traditional reactive risk models will not be adequate in the face of these new business demands. We will take a closer look at the risk management aspects of DSC in Chapter 7. The key reason it is deemed a waypoint on the leadership roadmap is that once the segment design is ready for implementation, it is imperative for leaders to think through risk implications before scaled-up deployment. Achieving transformational performance improvement cannot be considered successful if we are putting our own firm, or that of our value chain partners or customers, at material risk.

Case Example

Case: Multinational Manufacturer and Brand Marketer/ Retailor of Cosmetics

Industry and Competitive Landscape

For this case company, the senior leadership team issued a memo to its supply chain leaders about the new competitive reality the firm was facing. The memo highlighted increases in global competition, the need to find new ways to capture and create value, the need to become more integral to the overall firm's strategy execution, and the increased complexity of end-to-end operations. The need to act collectively, rather than individually was also communicated.

Organizational Situation

The leadership team then issued this call to action: The supply chain team will need to drive cost reductions of over 5% in the next 12 months. At the same time, they needed to retain their customer satisfaction and recommendations. They highlighted that they could not sacrifice quality in pursuit of efficiency. The need to improve operations was positioned as a way to improve customer loyalty, which would dive revenue improvements. They divided into three teams that would each take on various critical focus areas. The first team would focus on cost management and was charged with delivering a reduction in Cost of Goods Sold while reducing the cost of poor quality. The second team was charged with improving customer experience. They were asked to improved service levels and increase the on-time-in-full ratios. The last team was asked to focus on systems and process improvements. This meant improving order accuracy and implementing data governance and quality initiatives. The teams were asked overall to collaborate to meet their respective goals and at the same time build a supply chain of the future.

Leadership Response

The Power of Structured Dialog in Solving Supply Chain Problems

This case illustration replicates an example of the kind of problem-solving dialog that can be created with supply chain leadership programs designed to encourage collaborative problem solving. The quotations are actual comments (with identities hidden) made by executive education program participants in a leadership program that was delivered over the course of several weeks utilizing an online learning platform. Each subsection below represents a snapshot of program activities, as well as a curated excerpt of participant dialog associated with the program module. This sample dialog took place in one instance of a leadership program for approximately 40 supply chain executives in a global manufacturer and brand marketer of cosmetic products.

Activity One: Challenges and Opportunities in End-to-End Supply Chain
   In this exercise, participants were asked to identify one strength or vulnerability in their own segments of the supply chain. Having an E2E mindset is essential to developing a world-class supply chain

One participant wrote:

> *I think one way we could improve current forecasting is through a detailed historical data analysis. Not just looking at historical sales, but really digging into what made those sales and how those sales were made.*
>
> Director Purchasing & Production

Activity Two: Issues and Forces in Supply Chain

Discuss your perceptions of availability, adaptability, and affordability of our supply chain. Firm level challenges, and the landscape challenges of availability, adaptability, and the affordability of the supply chain.

In this next activity, another participant added to the idea around the details of sales forecasts with this comment:

> *the team has a many different individualized, ad-hoc models – no one is taking the same approach to create or evaluate their forecasts.*
>
> Assoc. Dir. Inventory Mgt.

Activity Three: Discuss One Supply Chain Strength or Vulnerability. How does this strength (or vulnerability) impact E2E?

> *I believe we can improve our forecasting by avoiding optimistic bias. Whenever I see the "excess list," I believe it is too long, and the items on it are taking up valuable space in our warehouse. If we had avoided optimistic bias, many of the items may not have ended up on the list.*
>
> Sr. Specialist Inventory Control

Activity Four: Competitive Implications of Demand Planning

Carrying inventory is expensive. Aligning incentives and developing an accurate forecasting model can help reduce inventories.

"*Recommendations to create alignment:*

- *Make sure all teams are aligned on company goal: "put the customer at the center"*
- *Segment the assortment*
- *Get alignment from the different teams on segmentation and define rules and goals for those groups*
- *Based on what the teams agree on (goals, rules, etc.), create reporting to measure progress and compliance*
- *Incorporate into bonuses.*" BREAKOUT GROUP 3

Activity Five: How Can You Improve Your Forecasting?

What can you do to improve forecasting? How would improved forecasting impact your role and customers?

> *A great point brought up by "Andy", people working together, functioning as one team, sharing best practices is a start. Involving the right people, trend and market analysis, and deep historical analysis, will help with forecasting accuracy and help with having the right products at the right place, at the right time.*
>
> Assoc. Director Sourcing

Activity Six: Forecasting and Inventory Management

How should you proceed? What ideas do you have about incentive alignment, inventory mgt, E2E recommendations?

> *We think that the main incentive for forecasting is driven by sales and the necessity to stay in stock. However, we need to be more strategic and strengthen our forecasting through market intelligence and determine if we met or exceeded our hurdle rate post launch. As a company we need to have a level of acceptance that being in an OOS position is more cost effective than having to expedite or putting ourselves at risk for having excess inventory.*
>
> BREAKOUT GROUP 6

Activity Seven: Demand Planning Live Event

Observations and decisions, estimates of stockout costs, forecasting at your company, alignment ideas

> *Our operation department goals should also not compete against each other as well. They should all be aligned for success and then the outliers only need addressing. This will create a robust end to end supply chain. Synergy is key. Changing the mindset and evolution is important as well. To not continue to follow a process just because it is what we always have done.*
>
> BREAKOUT GROUP 4

Activity Eight: Live Event: Critical Decisions – Wrap Up

Observations and decisions. Implications of course business challenge. Your cohort's learning and next steps

> *We're identifying more and more initiatives to increase value or reduce cost with more than $13,000,000 identified, and we were able to pull together a nice cross functional team about a week and a half ago to identify another $5,000,000 of additional stretched*

savings, which maybe if we weren't doing some of these cross-functional break-out, the team wouldn't have been as willing to share their ideas in a very cross functional way.

SVP Global Ops

Digital Supply Chain Case Questions

1. What do you think of this firm's approach to driving leadership behaviors and setting goals for itself?
2. Do you think this kind of leadership program could improve the degree of strategic alignment of supply chain associates across a global firm? Why or why not?
3. What are some examples of competitive threats that the case firm should be aware of? What kinds of digital supply chain strategies might they be competing with?
4. Is the case presenting challenges that are technology focused, or more about organizational behavior?
5. How much support do you think this firm's supply chain leadership exhibits towards accomplishing its stated goals and experience performance improvements?
6. Do you think a similarly designed leadership intervention might have similar impacts and outcomes in your own or other firms?

Summary

- Firms may mistakenly think that digital transformation starts with investments in technology. A better approach is to rapidly assess and test technologies to gain familiarity with them, adding them to a supply chain processes whose design calls for them.
- The DSC Leadership Road Map is designed to guide you through the numerous interrelated decisions about how to start your transformation process.
- Before embarking on the leadership road map, clearly define your digital transformation goals in terms of performance improvement targets. Your goals should ideally reduce the trade-offs between costs and customer satisfaction, enable new business models, and foster competitive advantage through hard to replicate integrated capabilities. It helps to continuously ask yourself and your team if your digital actions are aligned to these goals.
- The first step in the roadmap is determining "who are your customers", what are their characteristics, and how do we meet or exceed their expectations. This seemingly simple question has stumped many executives and is a highly effective starting point for most conversations about transformation.

- The second step is to determine the use of analytics to uncover segment opportunities. Ask yourself what the nonintuitive insights are you can develop about your customers and consumers. Nonintuitive insights are those that could not have been know without generating them from analysis.
- The third step is to design a new DSC segment, which will deliver the best supply chain for this segment, and enables business models that are innovative in meeting the customer needs.
- The fourth step is to review business models that integrate what we know about customers, in light of the data, technology, and processes at our disposal. The digital redesign of business models will require integrated support from senior leadership across business functions, increasing pressure on supply chain leadership.
- Step five is uncovering what talent, skill, and capabilities are needed to execute the new proposed design. Digital segment designs often require new talent as well as new relationships with internal functions, as well as external value chain partners.
- Step six is to determine which technologies are needed and available to execute the segment designs effectively. Leaders should be looking for strategic technology deployment that goes beyond automating an existing process and instead create new transformational business outcomes.
- The final step is to review what new business risks might be uncovered as a result of the new digital segment going into effect. Transformational performance cannot be considered successful if we put our own firm, value chain partners or customers at increased material risk.

References

Alaybayi, S., Linden, A., Rollings, M., & den Hamer, P. (2019). *Debunking Myths and Misconceptions About Artificial Intelligence. Gartner research note*, Jan 2019.

Bugihn, J., LaBerge, L., & Mellbye, A. (2017). *The case for digital reinvention. McKinsey Quarterly*, Feb 2017.

Ghosh, S. (2011, October 31). Developing a Supply Chain Leadership Mindset [Conference presentation]. Georgia Tech Scheller School of Business, Atlanta, GA, United States.

Lund, S., Manyika, J., Nyquist, S., Mendonca, L., & Ramaswamy, S. (2013). *Game changers: Five opportunities for US growth and renewal. McKinsey Global Institute, McKinsey & Company*, 1–158.

Wu, L., Yue, X., Jin, A., & Yen, D. (2016). Smart supply chain management: a review and implications for future research, *The International Journal of Logistics Management*, 27(2), 395–417

Xu, J. (2014). *Managing the Digital Enterprise*. Paris: Atlantis Press, 2014, doi:http://dx.doi.org/10.2991/978-94-6239-094-2.

5 Digital Supply Chain Talent and Organizational Strategies

Transforming into and running a Digital Supply Chain (DSC) requires firms to organize and behave in ways significantly different from the past. New business models, new data sources, new technologies, enhanced processes, and increased risks all contribute to an operational landscape that requires new ways of working and new skills to match; finding and recruiting new talent may not be enough. Bughun et al. (2019) argue that preparing people to manage across internal boundaries as the single most important aspect of digital transformation. Where can traditional firms uncover and attract digital talent? Are your recruiting strategies updated to account for your more digital competitors? Firms also face the reality that introducing bright new digital skills into traditional processes may not necessarily result in improvements in supply chain performance and meet resistance instead.

This chapter is about uncovering winning strategies for addressing the talent needs of firms undergoing digital transformation. In our conversations with supply chain leaders, we found that the digital "skills gap" was top of mind for all, yet few firms had begun to execute talent plans to address the challenge (Digital Supply Chain Institute [DSCI], 2020). This chapter will help you develop action plans to address the talent gap and accelerate your firm's transition into a DSC.

Given the recent major disruptions related to COVID-19, firms must ask themselves how these changes respond to talent and skills gap issues. In speaking to supply chain leaders, many indicated an immediate shift to online learning as a means of continuous learning and development during times of social distancing (DSCI, 2020). High-quality platforms are now available to enable effective social collaborative learning that is delivered virtually. Those interviewed also reaffirmed the increased importance of more integrated supply chain behaviors (DSCI, 2020). Development efforts must deliver action learning programs to support this shift in mindset including the inevitable shift of employment to more online fulfillment operations as a means of coping with the changes in customer behavior, as well as the displacement of supply chain associates.

Attacking the Problem – A DSC Talent Model

To address these issues, we developed a three-part talent model designed to guide research and provide a robust action-planning framework.

The three components of the model are as follows:

1.   Talent attraction and acquisition
2.   Talent development and skill-building
3.   Talent integration and performance improvement

1.   Attract and Acquire: Finding and Winning the Right Talent

This component looks at the way digitally savvy firms position themselves to attract new digital talent. The best performing companies revealed that specific actions were taken to signal to potential recruits that they were at the "right place" – the right company. Winning firms communicate that they value digital skills and offer more than a traditional transactional job. The roles these firms are seeking to fill focus on creative business problem-solving rather than simple technical skills. The best firms project an "Employment Brand" that is data-driven, community-oriented, and non-traditional, in ways that resonate with desirable, digital skill-rich candidates.

2.   Build and Develop: Developing Digital Talent and Skills

Once a firm has successfully attracted and recruited digital talent, plans must be put in place to develop their talent further. The firm must build upon the key skills talent will need for the specific business environment they will perform in, while developing employees as inter-company network performers. Such performance behaviors are not usually developed naturally; they require explicit capability building actions from firms. Building a culture and community of data-driven employees requires setting leadership examples and rewarding digital skill-building behaviors.

3.   Integrate and Perform: Driving Cross-Functional Integration and High Employee Performance

Developing a community of data-driven individual task performers is another key aspect of inciting a DSC transformation as new and innovative digital business models and segments, information and processes become highly integrated. In best-case examples, an "end-to-end" supply chain boasts seamless planning, sourcing, manufacture, and delivery to customers with business performance measured on high levels of customer satisfaction at managed costs. A well-crafted DSC talent plan necessitates organizational, not just individual, attributes. Integration involves organizational designs, employee mindset, and cross-functional behaviors. Supply chain transformation is about creating the conditions for higher levels of organizational performance and commitment.

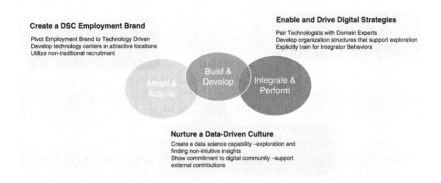

Create a DSC Employment Brand

Pivot Employment Brand to Technology Driven
Develop technology centers in attractive locations
Utilize non-traditional recruitment

Enable and Drive Digital Strategies

Pair Technologists with Domain Experts
Develop organization structures that support exploration
Explicitly train for Integrator Behaviors

Build &
Develop

Attract &
Acquire

Integrate &
Perform

Nurture a Data-Driven Culture

Create a data science capability –exploration and
finding non-intuitive insights
Show commitment to digital community –support
external contributions

Figure 5.1 Digital Supply Chain Talent Model.

Figure 5.1 shows the three main categories of the DSC Talent Model for action planning. The following are key insights for each of the model elements.

Key Insights and Implications for DSC Talent Planning

Talent and Organizational Strategy Key Insights: Attract and Acquire

- **Sourcing data science talent.** Many of the firms developing digital talent have invested serious effort in developing meaningful partnerships with universities in the fields of data science and data analytics. Partnerships include sponsoring and involving Ph.D. students in researching business problems for the firms, as well as developing curriculum. One key observation is much data-related talent is found outside of supply chain and business school programs and instead is sourced from math, statistics, and engineering departments.
- **New roles are being invented and developed.** Some firms are co-developing concepts of blended technical programs such as "data science engineering." This is a creative solution that attempts to address the real issue of data acquisition, cleansing, and alignment before creating and deploying data science models based on business understanding.
- **Leverage internally developed data science communities.** Firms described the importance of developing *Data Science Centers* or competency communities. Supply chain leaders should seek talent in such hubs and recruit them to focus on supply chain business challenges.

- **Consider looking outside the firm for key data talent.** Outsourcing, investment, and acquisition of firms with key talent are strategies that have been executed by firms seeking skills, especially for key data leadership roles.
- **Geography matters in talent strategies.** Recent research has shown that 60% of job growth is expected to occur in just 25 cities in the U.S. over the next decade. A large concentration of young, educated workers will be found in these hubs. It is possible that national talent acquisition strategies are too broad, and instead a regional approach in growth geographies is more appropriate (Bughun et al., 2019).
- **Look for talent outside your industry sector.** Some research suggests that supply chain knowledge is more transferable across industries than may be popularly thought. To increase your chances of finding needed talent, don't restrict yourself to only your firm's industry for experienced candidates (Alicke et al., 2017).
- Research has shown **disconnects between HR and Supply Chain** on competency requirements and hiring practices (Flöthmann et al., 2018).
- Become an **attractive employment brand** for data scientists, analytics engineers, and big data specialists and customer-centric process designers. Example: Wayfair's Technology blog at https://tech. wayfair.com/ illustrates an open communications channel that does more than just share tips for developers. If you look carefully at the images and ideas presented at this publicly available site, you will see employment branding at work. Images and profiles of current tech employees, diversity, work–life balance, and challenging collaborative work. Wayfair has been successful in recruiting thousands of data-savvy tech workers. You should take notice of how they address the talent market.
- **Develop an acquisition plan.** Evaluate your segmented DSC plans and prepare a skills gap inventory. Which skills are missing? What roles need to be filled? Target-specific skills needed for the segment strategy. Augment teams initially with outside consultants in data science, analytics, IoT, and so forth and learn what is specifically needed in your recruitment. Pair outside consultants with internal associates to improve knowledge transfer and development during digital pilots. Expand acquisition plans, communities, and networks based on pilot outcomes.

Attract and Acquire: Implications for Talent Planning

As you develop and evaluate your DSC Talent plans, consider the following questions:

- *Are you developing digital skills partnerships with universities and other sources of talent?*
- *Are you looking for the right skills? The right roles? Are roles described in ways that are up to date with the latest language and technologies?*
- *Are you creating and communicating a talent brand that is attractive to digitally skilled talent? Does your employment brand demonstrate a community of like-minded employees that is visible to talent prospects and recruiters?*
- *Do you have a plan for where to seek talent? Outside firms? The right geographies? The right sectors?*
- *Have you aligned your talent plants with your HR departments and clearly communicated your needs?*

Talent and Organizational Strategy Key Insights: Build and Develop

- Our research has shown that organizations should consider investing in the building of thoughtfully designed **data-centric supply chain communities** where co-located data-skilled talent works on supply chain problems. Data-centric skills, such as data engineering, data analytics, and data science, are best married to functional experts with experience in framing critical supply chain performance problems. By creating a working environment where technical skills and functional skills can collaborate on specific, clearly defined supply chain problems that are well chosen for urgency and impact, firms will reap the benefits of digital strategies more rapidly.
- **Learning & development is no longer a "nice to have."** Supply chain leaders no longer think of digital learning and development to be an optional investment (Alicke et al., 2017). Whether it is new talent that needs functional training in Supply Chain Management (SCM) or digital training to bolster the efficacy of supply chain "translators" who can blend functional and digital knowledge, the intersecting needs of staff all need development pathways to become more effective in executing digital strategies. There is a distinctive shift to support lifelong learning and an expectation that firms need to build a higher level of digital literacy among a broader range of associates. Recent studies have pointed out that production work and transportation services (supply chain positions) will have the highest job displacement rates (6 million jobs lost by 2030 in the U.S.) (Bughun et al., 2019). This will place additional pressure and urgency on the re-skilling plans of forward-thinking firms.
- **Be realistic** about the ability to re-train modest technicians into highly functioning analytic experts. The Digital Supply Chain

Institute's annual survey asked respondents, "how will you close the (digital) talent gap?" (DSCI, 2020). For the first time since the Institute began gathering this type of data, firms reported that the development of talent (57%) was the primary approach over the acquisition of talent (31%) (DSCI, 2020). This shift towards development brings with it some adjustments in expectations about which roles, skills, and types of development are feasible, and which transitions may be beyond reach. Developing supply chain analysts into data scientists, for example, may not be possible given the extensive education, dedication, and drive required for demanding technology roles. Also, managers should consider the array of needs in developing complex data-driven strategies. Our research has shown, for instance, that data scientists required to do all the data-engineering are a flight risk. Be sure to balance out development with current capabilities and be open to acquiring talent to fill key gaps.

- SCM and analytical problem-solving are key skills.

A recent study of 243 supply chain managers indicated that SCM managers involved in hiring ranked SCM knowledge and problem-solving skills as **three times** more important than general management skills (Flöthmann et al., 2018). This study allows us to better understand the competency requirements of supply chain planners and analysts and to identify personal preferences of hiring managers toward job candidates' competency profiles. The implications are that Human Resource Management and SCM experts should invest in joint efforts to define objective requirements to ensure a candidate's profile matches the needs, strategic goals, and organizational culture (Flöthmannet al., 2018).

- **Leadership Imperative.** Our research shows that new forms of digital-human interaction need thoughtful leadership attention. In one recent example, Walmart Inc. faced a strike by thousands of workers in South America in the wake of the retailer's push to increase automation at its physical stores (Lombrana, 2019). About 17,000 Walmart workers in Chile went on an indefinite strike in as many as 124 of the retailer's 375 stores across the country. The automation push "isn't Walmart's idea, it's the way our clients have decided to shop," said Monica Tobar, Walmart Chile Vice-president of Human Resources in an interview, "The world is going through a digital transformation and we need to be a part of that" (Lombrana, 2019). To avoid labor disruptions in operations, leaders need to approach human and digital interactions with greater sensitivity and preparation.

- **Plan for the displacement of associates who cannot survive the transition.** For associates whose skills have become out of date and are unwilling to undertake re-skilling to meet new job requirements, formulate a clear and transparent plan for their displacement.

- **Training should be targeted at service levels and needs simultaneously.** Development curricula should be created and published to show associates what they should be learning and offer direction on providers (internal vs. external) and the handling of training costs.

Build and Develop: Implications for Talent Planning

As you develop and evaluate your DSC Talent plans, consider the following questions:

- *Have you invested in and supported the development of supply chain knowledge communities where data-driven digital collaboration can grow?*
- *Are you developing and running digital leadership and functional learning programs that are accessible to the right staff? Are you taking advantage of these programs in ways that allow for cross-functional collaboration to be practiced and encouraged? Do your programs address the leadership aspects of transformation?*
- *Have you assessed the skills and capabilities of your current staff? Of your current teams, how many could be developed into more digital players and which do you think may need to be transitioned out?*
- *Are you clear about what skills are most needed for your DSC strategic implementation? SMC and analytic skills? Problem-solving skills?*

Talent and Organizational Strategy Key Insights: Integrate and Perform

- **Organizational considerations are critical in driving supply chain transformation.** In our research on talent, we focused on the acquisition of key talent needed for digital transformation, as well as aspects of the development of existing and newly acquired talent. In our data-gathering interviews with supply chain leaders responsible for digital transformation, higher levels of performance were found to depend on more than just the right sets of individuals. End-to-end supply chain performance requires both higher levels of integration across organizational functions, as well as possibly re-designing the interactions among functions. Kane et al. (2017) highlight the cultural as well as structural considerations when they point out that "leaders can't just command that the organization become more digital. They need to build a supportive culture that embraces collaboration, risk-taking, and experimentation" (p. 16).

- High-functioning individuals can unlock higher levels of performance, but their impact may be limited by inefficient organizational structures or lack of cross-functional collaboration.
- **Digital Talent Strategies must be aligned to digital transformation goals.** Talent acquisition, development, and integration plans should be tied to the overall DSC transformation strategies. Develop a segmented digital transformation plan, then develop a targeted set of skills needed to execute it. Talent plans may include outsourcing to consulting teams, recruitment, and tapping into shared organizational resources, among other things.
- **Firms should consider adopting** the same techniques used to create happy customers to facilitate productive employees. Recent literature has described the **"digital workforce"** as a concept that creates a positive employee experience. "Employee experience, (that is) the perceptions and feelings caused by complex interactions with colleagues, systems, and processes, has a powerful effect on performance" (Mann, 2019).
- **Organizational re-design to smaller, more agile business units.** Several firms have described their shifts away from hierarchal organizational designs towards smaller, independent, cross-functional business units. In one example, this organizational re-design led to a 70% reduction in lead times.
- **Digital projects have lifecycles.** Several interviewees mentioned that their DSC projects were not at all static in terms of skills required. Project life cycles demanded different skills during the problem definition, design, build and run phases. Interviewees also described the importance of integration behaviors which are not just skills and tools used by team members, but how team members interact with each other. One firm called the combination of role, skill, and interaction characteristics "personas." This is a rich characterization of the complexity of digital talent planning. It is a dynamic, complex leadership challenge to obtain the right mix of people to drive your digital strategies.
- **Digital projects still require standard project management approaches.** One firm warned digital adopters to not ignore the benefits of keeping transformational projects managed according to standard operating procedures. Having a formal innovation approach in place and supported by an existing innovation culture ensures that digital projects are deployed logically. Conventional project methods, such as assess, test, and deploy, are still relevant. The idea that digital is the new normal, and that projects are being implemented according to plans will create less

of a shock on employees compared with calling all digital projects "transformational." This idea is particularly important given some of the literature we have encountered which highlighted that the cultural adoption of an analytic mindset is overwhelming and difficult to manage for practitioners (Wieland et al., 2016). Perhaps the shift away from intuition-based decision-making to more analytic decision-making is a source of this discomfort.

- **People Performance Factors Matter.** Our research highlighted that firms could deploy algorithms to improve operational performance but must not ignore the psychological impacts of doing so on employees. More accurate digital forecasting may remove human biases and enhance operational performance, but the cultural adoption of predictive analytics may have barriers to implementation created by practitioners (DSCI, 2020).

Integrate and Perform: Implications for Talent Planning

As you develop and evaluate your DSC Talent plans, consider the following questions:

- *Does your DSC transformation plan adequately consider how your organizational structure promotes or inhibits integrated end-to-end behavior?*
- *Do you have a digital talent strategy that is explicitly linked to your segmented transformation goals?*
- *Do digital collaboration tools enable your workforce?*
- *Where does digital transformation start in the organization? Smaller agile business units? Broadly across multiple segments?*
- *Are you utilizing a rapid project life-cycle approach to implementing your DSC actions? Who do you have in place to staff these project teams? Do you have the right mix of talent and skills?*
- *Is there a standard project management approach to implementing DSC plans? Are project teams permitted to create their plans or align with an organizational approach?*
- *Are there human emotional considerations that may allow bias or create implementation barriers if left unaddressed?*

Taking Action: Key Insights for Talent and Organization

In summary, talent and organizational planning is a key driver of success for leading and implementing the DSC. We strongly advocate action planning now. Avoid the fate of many firms which recognize their talent plans are not up to the task and, at the same time, fail to move the needle on making progress. Some key leadership actions to initiate now are as follows:

Develop New (Non-Traditional) DSC Talent Plans

- Attract and retain scarce digital talent using new creative sourcing
- Evaluate your organizational culture as well as your current skills
- Build and interact with communities – pay attention to geographies – outside sectors
- Develop bold new roles now to harvest benefits in the future ("data science engineer") – SCM and problem-solving skills are still kings

Develop Action Plans and Set Goals

- Align with HR (research shows signs of misalignment)
- Pay attention to culture and build your employment brand
- Drive a *Leadership Imperative* involving digital human interactions
- Build communities – be realistic about training, but don't minimize the importance
- Develop and launch **purposeful training** that helps with skills, as well as attitudes and behaviors

Drive Performance and Action

- Develop organizational strategies to suit "new and different" or a "part of operating model" culture
- Consider creating smaller, independent, cross-functional Business Units to speed transformation
- Promote and reward integration behaviors critical to end-to-end digital implementation
- Recognize and counteract emotional responses to boundary spanning requirements that are "overwhelming and difficult to manage" for practitioners.

Organizational Structures

What should your initial organizational approach to developing your digital capabilities and outcomes look like? Decisions about centralization, decentralization, outsourcing, and organizational acquisitions require a target structure to ensure strategic alignment (Figure 5.2).

One approach is illustrated below. The guiding principles for this approach are as follows:

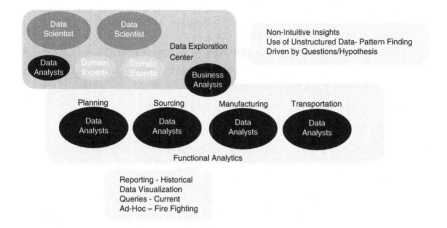

Figure 5.2 Example Organizational Approach.

- Data science is not the same as data analysis. Data science is strategically utilized to develop non-intuitive insights and patterns in an exploratory manner. Analytics are less exploratory and predictive, and, therefore, require a skill set that is more directed to functional reporting.
- As an initial approach, try to develop a small "Data Exploration Center" that is centralized and whose direction is set by enterprise strategy. Rare and expensive, top data science talent should be protected from more mundane data engineering (quality and cleansing) tasks and focused instead on business-specific scientific questioning and hypothesis testing for the enterprise.
- Data analytics talent may be decentralized and aligned with functional performance reporting.

Key Role Definitions

Data Scientist Profile

- **Highly skilled, highly trained** individuals experienced in building sophisticated analytic models with explanatory power, as well as predictive power.
- Data Scientists are capable **data modelers**, evaluators of **data quality**, data miners, mathematicians, statisticians, and computer programmers often rolled into one **unique** person. They often define business problems and **explore** hypotheses utilizing data rather than creating reports.
- Data Scientists are comfortable working with **high volume data** sets, high velocity, and a wide variety of both **structured and unstructured**

data. They can ascertain the relevancy of disparate data sources and find ways to connect them with **integrity and validity** in search of answers to **complex problems.**

- Data Scientists can be **rare and difficult to recruit and retain** and are drawn to top digital native organizations such as Amazon and Google, who they feel may better value their unique capabilities.

Data Steward Profile

- **Data stewards** are individuals who have a key responsibility in championing, sponsoring, or ensuring data quality, integrity, alignment, and analytic availability.
- **Data stewards** must **understand** and **influence** key business processes that generate transactional data, as well as safely replicate and allow for the access of analytic data stores to the firm's data consumers.
- **Data stewards** are responsible for the key **strategies/structures** that **enable** enterprise data dictionaries, cross-functional data definition and changes, data analytics, and warehousing processes, such as extraction and transformation, as well as data set duplication for analyst consumption.

Data Engineers Profile

Data Engineers are responsible for:

- Key **actions/processes** that enable the effective design of enterprise-wide data dictionaries
- Cross-functional data definition and changes, data analytics and warehousing processes, such as the extraction, transformation of data formatting, and loading or alignment to data stores and lakes
- Data Quality and Alignment
- Data provisioning for analyst consumption
- Data lake architecture, development, and deployment

Chapter 5 Case Example

Multinational Manufacturer and Brand Marketer of Packaged Foods

Industry and Competitive Landscape

The packaged foods industry has become increasingly competitive in many segments. The case company occupies a top position in several easily recognizable consumer categories such as breakfast cereals, backing goods, grain-based snacks and others. Several of its top categories have recently experienced some downturn due to changes in consumer buying habits. Consumer health trends such as increased preference for whole grains and reduced sugars are examples. Increased competition from organic and private label specialty store brands has also increased pressure on revenue, volumes, and margins. Product innovation to remain relevant to the new consumer also has been critical. Private label specialty brands have provided a high degree of downward pricing pressure with some product categories selling for significantly less than those prices enjoyed some few years earlier.

Organizational Situation

The case company knows that their future success demands that they get more from their manufacturing sites. Growth is hard to come by, and it is extremely critical that they get more from their assets moving forward and so if growth is slower, they need to extract more production from their asset base. If growth accelerates, they need to defer capital to create organic food capacity. Senior leadership for supply chain feels that it is very important that supply chain associates understand the cultural shifts and business strategies of the firm, focused on intelligent and enterprise wide efficiency. The firm named this combination strategy "Value Stream Culture" or "VSC." The firm's supply chain has historically been manufacturing-centric, with many KPIs focused on cost per unit produced. This drove behaviors of full and long production cycles with few changeovers. To enable agility and growth, the firm's supply chain leadership feels that a more enterprise margin management mindset is needed, one that optimizes value stream processes over functional measures. Functions are incentivized to optimize their own performance at the expense of the broader value stream. Supply chain leadership feels that a value stream orientation will force a set of activities and processes that enable good quality trade-off decisions. VSC, along with specific firm-focused leadership behaviors, is intended to directly enable the employee engagement mindset necessary to enact the growth strategy. Supply chain leadership also feels that the culture of the firm needs to move to a greater degree of awareness of how supply chain actions impact downstream measures, particularly Return on Invested Capital (ROIC). No one currently owns the value stream. Supply chain leadership therefore feels that VSC must be enabled and activated at scale within the global supply chain organization.

Market Trends Impacting Business Performance

Firm leadership identified the following business performance issues as the immediate need to:

- Reignite Growth of Traditional Product Categories
- Enable Growth of New Product Categories (i.e., Organics and Natural – health-oriented categories)

To address these challenges, leadership also defined key leadership focus areas that they felt the supply chain must adopt to support the business conditions and growth objectives. They are:

- Build "VSC" – which is comprised of reducing waste, human and food Safety, and end-to-end performance improvement
- Breaking Down of Functional Silos – plan, source, make and deliver have different leadership, metrics, and business drivers
- Supply Chain Agility – ability to adapt and move supply chains away from traditional to those more driven by customer and consumer trends, demand and behavior

Leadership Response

In this case, the supply chain leaders realized that they needed to encourage their associates to develop new ways of working that included shifts in mindset and attitude, as well as changes to processes and technology. Some of the leadership enablers identified for development included servant leadership, which focused on building trust, accessibility, and the removal of barriers between functional and boundary spanning processes. Additionally, the firm recognized the need to build an active waste reduction mindset based on self-motivation, individual inspiration, and engagement, rather than top down directives. The firm realized that cross-functional integration behaviors and the active creation of more holistic cost management were something that needed direct attention through the building of cultural awareness.

DSC Implications – Actions

The case firm created leadership development programs that were focused on:

- Basic understanding and education about the VSC
- Building a strong culture of employee engagement, process rigor, and leadership
- New and renewed awareness of metrics on human safety/ environment and food safety
- Optimized end-to-end margin management outcomes including firm-specific metrics on reliability, logistics, and customer service levels

The leadership program intervention was given a name to build its own brand awareness inside the firm. Example program titles were as follows:

> Identifying the Forces Shaping Your Supply Chain: *Breaking down silos and functional mindsets*
> Finding Value in Your End-to-End Supply Chain: *Identifying sources of value creation, ROIC and cost savings in your organization*
> Driving to Perfect Order: *Delivering the Perfect Order at sustainable costs and working capital with fewer quality trade-off decisions*

DSC Readiness

The language used by the firm echoes some of the key strategic tenants of the DSC but does not tend to use any of the terms currently associated with the field. Traditional metrics are at the forefront. There is noticeably little mention of data and or analytics as sources of insight generation or strategy development. Segments are discussed mostly in terms of larger categories, like "organics," rather than on more detailed segments like "adult, health-oriented breakfast cereals." There seems to be an entrenched devotion to existing business models with innovation being focused on product and packaging innovation, rather than new ways to service customers. Risk management is highly focused on human and food safety, which makes sense. Since there do not seem to be DSC actions under discussion, digital risks seem quite remote currently.

If you were brought into this firm to help with its strategic rethinking of its supply chain, what digital roadmap would you recommend they start with? Is a large-scale organizational level initiative likely given the investments this firm is already making in leadership and VSC mindset?

Digital Supply Chain Case Questions

1. What kind of digital supply chain segment strategies might help the case company improve in its stated metrics and goals?
2. What are some examples of competitive threats that the case firm should be aware of? What kinds of digital supply chain strategies might they be competing with?
3. Is the case presenting challenges that are technology focused, or more about organizational behavior?
4. Are there individual oriented interventions that will move the needle on the firm's business challenges?
5. How much support do you think this firm's supply chain leadership

will need in order to accomplish its stated goals and experience performance improvements?

6. What is the difference between a "value stream" and a supply chain?
7. What can supply chain do to help create more innovative products that will delight customers, increase satisfaction, and increase revenues?

Summary

- Digital transformation requires human capital to manage the supply chain end-to-end across organizational boundaries. This means that firms will have to organize and behave in ways significantly different from the past.

- While the digital skills gap is top of mind for executives at many firms, few have begun to execute talent plans that are explicitly designed to meet the challenge. New efforts to develop talent are needed to address both transformation initiatives, as well as meet immediate needs.

- To address these issues, we have developed a three-part talent model to guide research, as well as provide a robust action-planning framework. The three components of the model are as follows: (1) talent attraction and acquisition, (2) talent development and skill-building, and (3) talent integration and performance improvement.

- To be effective in attracting and acquiring talent, firms need to take specific actions to communicate that they value digital skills and offer more than a traditional transactional job. The best firms project an "employment brand" that is data-driven, welcomes diversity, is community-oriented, and non-traditional.

- Once a firm has acquired the right talent, it needs to have plans for how to build individual skills as well as network collaboration skills. Building a culture and community of data-driven employees requires leadership setting examples by rewarding digital skill-building behaviors.

- The digital end-to-end supply chain strives to become more seamless in planning, sourcing, manufacturing, and delivery to customers. Enabling this seamless digital supply chain transformation requires leading the creation of conditions for more integrated organizational behaviors.

- Digital supply chain talent strategies and plans will make decisions about centralization, decentralization, outsourcing, and acquisitions including those that require revised and aligned organizational structure.

- Data scientists, stewards, and engineers are roles that are often unclear in lay-person conversations about talent in organizations. The best firms and leaders will educate themselves about the differences between digital roles to allow for greater clarity in talent management and performance.

References

Alicke, K., Dumitrescu, E., Leopoldseder, M., & Sankur, A. (2017, July). Digital supply chains: Do you have the skills to run them? *McKinsey & Company.* https://www.mckinsey.com/business-functions/operations/our-insights/digital-supply-chains-do-you-have-the-skills-to-run-them#

Bughun, J., Manyika, J., & Woetzel, J. (2019, July). The future of work in America. *McKinsey Global Institute.* https://www.mckinsey.com/featured-insights/future-of-work/the-future-of-work-in-america-people-and-places-today-and-tomorrow

Digital Supply Chain Institute. (2020). Talent & organizational planning: A guide to closing the digital supply chain skills & performance gap [white paper]. *Center for Global Enterprise.* Retrieved from https://www.dscinstitute.org/assets/documents/2020-DSCI_Talent_Guide.pdf

Flöthmann, C., Hoberg, K., & Weiland, A. (2018). Competency requirements of supply chain planners and analysts and personal preferences of hiring managers. *Supply Chain Management: An International Journal, 23*(6), 480–499. https://doi.org/10.1108/SCM-03-2018-0101

Kane, G., Palmer, D., Phillips, A., Kiron, D., Buckly, N. (2017). Achieving digital maturity. *Slone Review MIT, 59*(1), 1–29.

Lombrana, L. M. (2019, July 10). Walmart workers rebel against retailer's robot push in Chile. *Bloomberg.* Retrieved from https://www.bloomberg.com/news/articles/2019-07-10/walmart-workers-rebel-against-retailer-robot-push-in-chile

Mann, J. (2019, April 26). A digital workplace is crucial to digital transformation. *Gartner Research.* Retrieved from https://www.gartner.com/en/doc/3909082-a-digital-workplace-is-crucial-to-digital-transformation

Mehta, A., & Mehta, N. (2017). Knowledge integration and team effectiveness: A team goal orientation approach. *Decision Sciences, 49*(3), 445–486. https://doi.org/10.1111/deci.12280.

Meyer, M. (2017). The supply chain workforce of the future. *Supply Chain Management Review, 21*(4), 18–23. Retrieved from https://www.scmr.com/article/the_supply_chain_workforce_of_the_future

Wieland, A., Handfield, R., & Durach, C. (2016). Mapping the landscape of future research themes in supply chain management. *Journal Of Business Logistics. 37*(3), 205–212.

6 Digital Supply Chain Technology Management

This chapter covers a strategic overview of the most critical technologies utilized by the digital supply chain (DSC). Advancements in Internet of Things (IoT) and sensors, artificial intelligence and machine learning, generative design, robotics, 3D printing, and driverless transportation are some of the most potentially disruptive (LeVine, 2019; Lohr, 2012; Lopez & Andrews, 2019; Majeed & Rupasinghe, 2017). Supply chain leaders cannot afford to have a superficial understanding of these technologies if they are to remain competitive. We will discuss, in practical terms, what is unique and significant about these advances, as well as leadership actions that should be taken over different time horizons. Note that we have created a glossary of many of the technical terms mentioned here and it is included in this volume.

For leaders to be successful, they should adhere to a few of the key strategic goals and objectives of managing digital technologies in the supply chain:

- Strategically utilize digital technology to improve supply chain performance
- Continually evaluate application of new technologies and data sources, integrating for customer segments as appropriate
- Utilize technology generated data to effectively understand past performance and predict future demand and risks
- Use technology in creative, connected, and integrated ways to unlock new "hard to replicate" business models that delight customers and consumers

These goals define what good technology management is and should drive leadership actions. To be "connected and integrated" is especially intriguing in our current environment and to illustrate what is different and powerfully new about this idea, we have developed an example using an athletic shoe product from UnderArmour (UA). This example is meant to be illustrative, not specific. It is loosely based on real technology strategies deployed by UA but was created as a learning tool.

Also note that the business case example is very much in real-life flux, with recent reports of the possible sale of all or part of the connected shoe infrastructure[1]. None of this should change the main points about the case and the learning points contained therein. We are seeking to discover possibilities in this chapter. Evaluating business results and capturing real market share and revenues are the ultimate business goals, but before we get there we have to be able to envision what an integrated technology approach looks like.

The Story of the Internet Connected Running Shoe

When we teach this example in executive education programs, we start with a story about the renowned Venkat Venkatraman, now a professor at Boston University. Venkat, as he is known, describes himself as a "strategist and futurist[2]" and is the author of book "The Digital Matrix – New Rules for Business Transformation Through Technology." The story takes us back to 1999, which in technological terms is a lifetime, and an executive education audience of PwC partners at London Business School. Venkat was presenting on technology strategy to the partners, who at the time were just beginning to grapple with the new implications of the internet and business. In one case example, Venkat described a future where there would likely be sensors built into consumers' shoes. The sensors would gather and transmit data about the wearers' health and fitness and be aggregated and analyzed by future internet business firms. This idea, presented to the senior partners of the global accounting firm, was met with some degree of respectful humor and skepticism. How interesting it is to reflect on this now, as we have had commercially available shoes with these very sensors of the future for the last several years! Our advice, therefore, is to pay close attention to what Venkat foresees for the *next* 20 years.

This brings us to our current case and it is safe to say at least a few of the technologies in this example were not even dreamed of 20 years ago when it was still "Day 1[3]" for the internet. The story now shifts to the Lighthouse Manufacturing and Design Leadership Center[4] of UA, which is a laboratory and experimental station for product innovation and development for the athletic consumer product manufacturer.

From HOVR to ArchiTech, a Technology Evolution

Since we mentioned sensors in shoes, let's pick up the story with the UA HOVR connected shoe, which is built with "Record Sensors™" that track, analyze, and store numerous running metrics for the individual wearer. Some of the sensor data generated for the athlete are running cadence, distance, pace, stride, and steps. The UA brand is about improving the consumer's athletic performance, so the added features of the sensor data are intended to generate demand from the running enthusiast segment. This kind of product that features sensors that generate and transmit data to further enhance customer services are typically called "connected" products. In the case of UA's HOVR, the data generated from the shoes are relayed to an iOS and Android mobile phone app called MapMyRun™. MapMyRun™ acts as a controller, receiver, and analyzer of the data generated by the shoe mounted Record sensors. Once the HOVR sensors are linked to the user's MapMyRun™ app, its user interface and code generate and store performance information for running activities. Users can review distance, duration, average pace, average stride length, cadence (steps per minute), and calories burned. To recap the product story so far, athletic runner consumers can synchronize their connected sensor-embedded shoes to a personal analytic application to easily review their activities while wearing the configured connected product.

Next Up: Performance Coaching

If HOVR shoes only offered simple personal feedback reporting on the data collected, this would be considered a value-added product feature for many consumers. Being a connected product means that data collected on an individual level is also transmitted back to servers associated with the application developer and host. UA is able to gather and analyze, in a more centralized manner, the activity data from customers using the HOVR and MapMyRun™. This ability to gather data directly from the end-user consumer is a cornerstone of digital business. Rather than product sales to consumers being a one-way street, the connected product experience allows for information to be shared in both directions, directly between the consumer and brand manufacturer. No matter how the shoes are sold to the consumer, e-commerce retail, specialty retailer, brand owned retail stores, it is striking that once the connected product is set-up, communications and information are able to become frictionless between the brand and consumer. The implications of this nascent development are enormous. Imagine what it would mean for increasing numbers of product categories to be equipped with this capability. Knowledge of consumers and their usage habits for products goes to a whole new level. Consumption patterns of all types can be imagined, all giving the brand manufacturer new levels of analytic power with which to adjust its products, services, and supply chains.

Returning to the UA story, this growing knowledge base of athletic performance behavior at the UA labs enables a number of strategic actions. The first is that UA is able to extend the product service package for the consumer by offering individuals feedback about their running activities. UA compares the individual data for a runner against the data generated and researched by its athletic coaches and data scientists. This service manifests itself for the consumer through an app-delivered feature called "Real-Time Form Coaching." The idea behind this feature is to "help runners reduce risk of injury and make running feel easier."[5] This part of the product value proposition obviously goes far beyond simply protecting a runner's feet while running. The value-added benefits also align directly to the UA brand by helping its athletic consumers perform better. The app features also include social media type connects where runners can share data and challenge each other, as well as create training plans for 5K races or marathons. UA has added another extension to this concept by partnering with Samsung and its wearables product business. As of this writing, UA has developed technology integration with the Samsung Galaxy watch (Garmin and Apple watches are also supported). This device also has heath-based sensors that gather and communicate real-time and post-activity feedback on parameters such as heart rate, blood pressure, emergency fall detection, and GPS map integration.

It's a dizzying array of data points for individuals and creates the possibility of pooling data from large numbers of users to open up even more business possibilities.

What Large Amounts of Meaningful Data from Consumers Means for Supply Chains

While one objective of providing added connected services to consumers is to enhance the product experience and value proposition, there are also strategic supply chain opportunities created by building a connected product data base. One way in which better insights into consumer behavior and product usage data could benefit supply chain performance is through more timely and accurate demand forecasts. In our UA example, we should have a good idea, based on the number of runs, length, conditions, steps, and so forth, when a pair of running shoes will need replacement. Making personal offers to consumers that reduce the friction of the replenishment transaction is attractive to both the brand and the consumer. From a consumer standpoint, I may begin to feel some larger switching costs once my shoe purchases are linked to more than the product itself. Now I stand to lose my running history and plans, coaching, and social connections should my new replacement pair of shoes not link to my existing data and app. There is value in being alerted to when the physical performance of my shoes may be dwindling as well. A push reminder and offer, direct from the brand, makes it easier and more satisfying to keep my running habit going. From the brand perspective, there are some intriguing additional benefits as a connected product relationship has been established providing the firm with a legitimate chance at forging a direct-to-consumer business. Irrespective of where the consumer purchased the initial connected product, online data connections and service streams between the brand and consumer create new advantage disintermediating retailers and distributors. The brand is in the best position, based on its knowledge about the consumer, to satisfy their needs for the category. The supply chain can, in this model, be a source of driving demand and revenues, rather than simply fulfilling orders from distributors and retailers.

We have discussed the positive business impacts of improving the supply chain's ability to forecast in a more timely and accurate way, direct manufacturing resources, manage inventories, and optimize transportation and storage costs amongst other things. What could supply chain leaders do if they utilized consumer-level product usage and behavioral data to collaborate with product innovation designers and new manufacturing techniques? What if these processes were, in fact, connected to the rich and voluminous data stores that are being produced, and enriched each day by connected product end users?

The Game-Changing Technology of Generative Design

Generative design is touted as the killer app of the supply chain. As a result of well-modeled technology being fed large volumes of relevant, high quality data, it becomes possible to produce manufactured product designs that are beyond human capabilities. As supply chain leaders it is critical to understand the strategic value of algorithmic generative design and to determine if there is a use case for it in your product design and manufacturing processes. The power of the machine-based process to generate millions of possible design outcomes based on constraints and outputs has already created products and engineering components that appear to have been designed through organic evolutionary processes. The designs resemble complex natural organic forms and are practically impossible to manufacture by techniques other than 3D printing. Such was the case for UA when their engineers and designers went to work in the UA Lighthouse to take the HOVR shoe concept several generations further in its evolution.

Big Data + Generative Design +3D printing = A Totally New Kind of Product

The UA example boasts the number one asset to enhance the use of generative design algorithms in design and manufacturing: a large source of actual end-user performance data. The key to this story is the pool of sensor-based data generated by and freely submitted to UA for design analysis and algorithmic training. In some published examples, engineers place sensors on a modified existing product and gather data points during test runs. This sample data set is then fed into the generative design algorithm along with constraints to create design output options. Machine learning accuracy, however, depends on large volumes of data created under a wide variety of real-world conditions. This is exactly what HOVR and MapMyRun do for UA.

There are, of course, limitations to the use of generative design processes and some obvious reasons why it is not the blanket solution for design problems where aesthetics are more critical than performance. In the UA case, the ultimate generative design output was optimized for athletic performance, not aesthetics. The new shoe design was intended for athletes who are interested in, and willing to pay for, a performance edge from their equipment. This culture of performance over looks has many examples in the sport of running. It is not uncommon for runners to take knives to their running shoes to improve their fit, flexibility, and traction. Another example is the continued niche popularity of unfashionable running shorts which are perfect for the unrestricted movement needed to improve running performance but are horribly out of place in a restaurant or family gathering. As we have seen, it is all about best meeting the needs of your customer segment.

The Design Outcome: The 3D Printed UA ArchiTech Shoe

The UA team, armed with user-level running data, Autodesk generative design software, and 3D printing equipment, prototyped a new kind of futuristic running shoe, called the UA 3D ArchiTech. The shoe's mid-sole looks like a complex web of flexible interconnecting rods and channels, unlike anything else UA had ever designed with human designers. The 3D ArchiTech will be outfitted with UA Record sensors, similar to the HOVR, to gather end-user feedback about the prototype's performance. Imagine a development loop of printing, then making prototypes and measuring performance in the real world, iterating further on the growing body of design knowledge. Once a baseline design is established based on the large volumes of Big Data from users, how hard would it be for UA to establish a bespoke, custom printed ArchiTech pair for high-performance segment enthusiasts based on unique running attributes, habits, and form parameters? For customers willing to pay for this individualized performance product to gain a competitive edge, this may not be far beyond the realm of possibility. After-market orthotics, a helpful add-on for many runners may become obsolete as the shoes themselves can be manufactured for a customer of one, taking into considerations their unique physical needs.

What Does This Supply Chain System Look Like?

For one of our recent executive education programs, we created a one-page chart to illustrate the interconnections of the UA example which is shown in Figure 6.1. Some additional potential data points of social

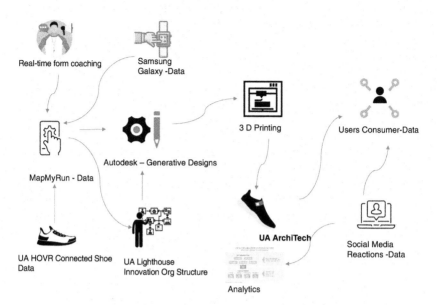

Figure 6.1 UnderArmour ArchiTech Example (From a lecture by Kurz, 2020).

media reactions to the shoes as they are marketed were added to complete the picture. Commercially, the ArchiTech is still limited to prototypes as of this writing. At the prototype stage, a pair of ArchiTech shoes are prohibitively expensive to all but the most dedicated athletes. By sharing this example, the hope is that supply chain leaders will begin to think in a more integrated way across a user experience landscape when they re-imagine or design their DSCs. In one of our executive leadership programs, we had Craig Jones, UA's Head of Supply Chain join us and we asked him for his reaction to the chart, first to see if we had the key components characterized correctly. To our relief Craig confirmed that it was basically correct for the purposes of describing the design and development strategy. The next key point that emerged in our discussion came from looking across all of the various departments, functions, data sources, technologies, talent, and feedback loops that are needed to bring this particular DSC to life. This picture, complex in some ways, and elegant in others, characterizes the leadership challenges supply chain executives face when seeking digital transformational performance outcomes. The relationships, influence, negotiations, interdependence, collaboration, and, ultimately, integration needed to bring the DSC to life is absolutely a leadership challenge.

Taking the Next Steps – What Actions Can Leaders Take Now?

To conclude this chapter, we will continue to develop the framework to assist in the process of planning DSC transformation actions. In Figure 6.2, we have pictured a DSC Technology Maturity Model. The purpose of this model is to help leaders assess and plan for strategic improvement actions in technology. Horizon one is the current landscape and environment, which keeps operations running smoothly. Just beyond this horizon is the Growth horizon which is perhaps 9–18 months out from our current operations. Actions taken in the Growth horizon enable the capture of revenues or reduced costs not currently in our grasp. Beyond this, horizon three, which is perhaps a few years out from the current operation, is called the Transformation horizon. It's aspirational, yet realistic.

Leadership Actions to Drive Digital Transformation

The maturity map illustrates a few key technology leadership ideas. The first is to be strategic, rather than opportunistic, when assessing technology needs. Developing capabilities and running pilot projects should be focused on critical issues, gaps in execution, competitive threats, and supporting new digital segment designs. Technology should be evaluated and prioritized before scaling it to enterprise levels, and your technology investments should align to your business strategy (Michel, 2017;

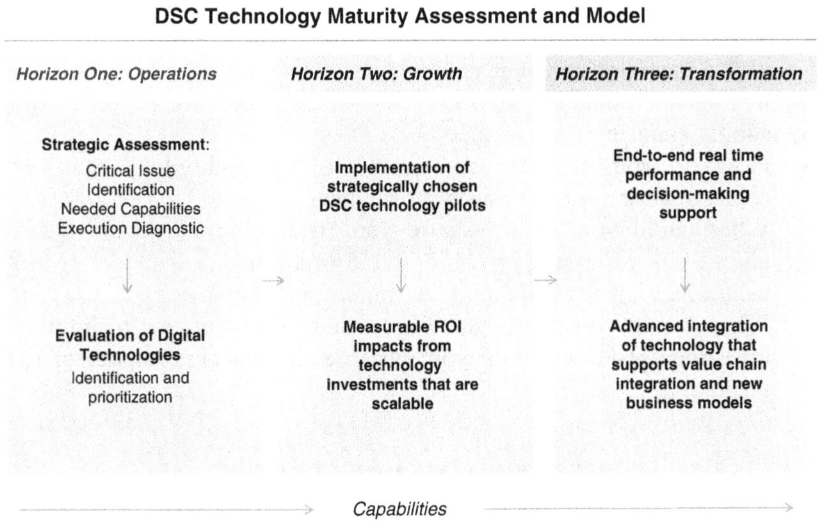

DSC Technology Maturity Assessment and Model

Horizon One: Operations	*Horizon Two: Growth*	*Horizon Three: Transformation*
Strategic Assessment: Critical Issue Identification Needed Capabilities Execution Diagnostic	Implementation of strategically chosen DSC technology pilots	End-to-end real time performance and decision-making support
Evaluation of Digital Technologies Identification and prioritization	Measurable ROI impacts from technology investments that are scalable	Advanced integration of technology that supports value chain integration and new business models

Capabilities

Figure 6.2 Technology Maturity Horizon Map for Technology.

Walker et al., 2018). Horizon one should be heavy on planning and lighter on deployment of new operating technology.

In the Growth horizon, strategically chosen technology pilots can be deployed, along with specific metrics, for measuring business improvement outcomes. Projects and deployments that show targeted levels of return on investment may be planned for scaling up. Finally, in the Transformation horizon we expect to see technology deployments that improve DSC performance. Improvements in reducing information latency, more end-to-end integration, and the enablement of new business models supporting targeted segments.

Leadership Tools – Guiding Questions for You and Your Teams

As introduced in Chapter 3, the following are a set of management questions to pose to yourself and your teams in a guided fashion. We have used these questions to help guide executive education participants through the complex thought processes of transforming into and leading digital businesses. We present them here as a resource to consider as we close this chapter on technology management.

Driving Questions – Technology Management

- Will the deployment of digital technologies enable new business models for your firm? If not, can you think of ways it could? If so, what leadership actions should you take to drive changes in your firm's business models?
- What actions could you and your team take to more effectively utilize emerging relevant technologies such as blockchain, artificial intelligence, machine learning, 3D printing, etc. to improve your supply chain performance?
- How do you maintain awareness of new technology that can enhance your supply chain performance?
- What could you do to ensure your technology investments are aligned to your supply chain transformation strategy? How are technology investments made within your company?
- What would you do to make a business case for new technology investments? How would you measure the business impact of the results?

Concluding Thoughts on Technology Leadership

The key technology leadership challenge facing many firms is gaining sufficient traction to convene functionally integrated technology strategies across the organization (Paley, 2017). For many projects, persuasive leadership is required to recruit, motivate and engage organizational partners in boundary spanning technology collaboration and subsequent sharing of data. If e-commerce platforms gather data from consumers useful to manufacturing, how can leadership ensure that the information spreads across the organization to create impact? Sophisticated management models should go beyond rudimentary data sharing and find ways to design and implement integrated technology solutions that are potentially end-to-end in nature.

Case Example

Case: Multinational Manufacturer and Brand Marketer of Pharmaceuticals

Industry and Competitive Landscape

Pharmaceutical research, development, manufacturing, and distribution firms have faced something of a supply chain shock over the last decade. As regulatory protections lifted for generic competition, the fundamentals of supply chain for big pharma companies changed dramatically (Ehrhardt et al., 2014). As high grossing blockbuster drugs come off patent protection, generics have eaten deeply into drug margins, which has had a direct impact on supply chain performance. Think about it. If you have a lock on a particular drug in the market, and the pricing and margins are very high, often serious multiples over cost, the strategy of the supply chain is to carry high levels of inventory, so that the firm rarely experiences a stock-out situation. The carrying costs of the high inventory levels are easily absorbed into the high profit margins afforded the monopoly market product. As regulations changed, and the famous "patent cliff" emerged for pharma, those cushy margins evaporated. A drug that used to enjoy a margin of $70 per pill might see a drop to a margin of $.07 a pill under the competitive pressure of a generic alternative. The supply chain implications of this change are profound. The supply chain systems, behaviors, large-batch manufacturing runs, logistics, and flexibility were all tailored to a high margin, less lean design. To remain competitive in this new business environment, pharma supply chains needed to become more segment focused, flexible, connected to value chain partners, and more accurate in planning and forecasting. That's a lot of change in a short amount of time. This has created pressure on pharma supply chain leaders to develop effective transformation plans that can overcome technical, and cultural barriers.

Organizational Situation

Our case company is a large, diversified, multinational, multi-business unit, pharma research, development, marketing, sales, and distribution company. It is the definition of "Big Pharma". It hosts thousands of different supply chains, each to some degree tailored to the needs of hospitals, patients, third-party payors, consumers, and pharmaceutical retailers. In order to deal with this complex transformational challenge, the case firm first established what it felt were the key attributes of a best-in-class supply chain. Many of the attributes will sound familiar, they are:

1. End-to-End Visibility including data visibility, as well as physical inventory visibility that consolidates information across enterprise wide sources data
2. Market channel differentiation which means understanding the needs of different channels, such as retail, hospital, distributors, and direct to consumer. Knowing how competitors interact and serve these channels as well as segment differentiation within them.
3. Rapid innovation capability in both manufacturing processes to meet new market needs for flexibility as well as business process innovation to better serve channels and segments.
4. End-to-end process improvements that reduce trade-offs between inventory vs. service levels, and quality vs. cost. This attribute will also strive to link functional priorities to business unit strategy

Leadership Response

Supply chain leadership at the case company rallied around the need to develop an enterprise level strategy to stand as a proxy for numerous efforts to improve across the best in class attributes. In an effort to consolidate many complex attributes into one programmatic brand, the company named the enterprise strategy. For the purposes of this case we will call this the "Proxy Strategy" (PS). The PS stood for integrated processes, technologies, data, customer insights that all were focused on DSC performance improvement. The aim was to build a culture around the PS, and a normalization of developing and executing efforts in support of it. The supply chain leadership felt this would be less of a shock culturally than branding these initiatives in terms of digital transformation.

The case company also viewed the PS as serving customer sectors and segments within sectors. Each segment was focused on customer needs, as well as new potential and adjacent data and information flows that might help pinpoint segment actions.

In sector-based approach – segments within sectors – customer voice is central to prioritization of portfolio. For example, the supply chain leadership was careful to rethink and further define standard supply chain measures, such as On-Time-In-Full (OTIF) as it is defined by customers in segments, not based on internal metric definitions. The OTIF-customer metric was also validated in partnership and collaboration with commercial sales colleagues.

Next supply chain leadership sought to systematically review data resources for key processes, ensuring there was alignment between physical and information flows. In this process they found that some segments were well aligned and others that needed remediation. The key point here is that these reviews should be conducted on a segmented basis and that there may not be one blanket action that is needed or beneficial for all segments concurrently. Assessment of the current state is critical.

Remediation was split into data actions, as well as physical actions. Digital data included data science, analytics, and data visualization, while physical platform innovation focused on elements of 3D printing, robotics, and other types of automation.

Focus on Digital Talent

In this case example, the firm recognized the need for a new approach to talent development for the DSC, investing in specific program, academies, and third-party vendors to develop specific capabilities that were identified as upskillable and designated skills for outside procurement. Data science, for instance, was deemed an outside procurement skill; therefore, there were no plans to attempt to train engineers to be data scientists. The firm invested in building a centralized data science center in an offshore country where teams would be assigned to work on various company strategies.

While the firm was focused on making key strategic leadership hires at the highest level, it was also investing in upskilling talent. Improving its functional domain experts in the language and strategic capabilities of data science so that they could act as interpreters, bridging the needs of functions with the capabilities of the centralized data scientists. The first also worked to build a culture of data specialists who would act as data governance citizens, helping to create a culture of data quality and integrity for the firm.

DSC Implications – Actions

In spite of the size and complexity of this case company example, they seem to exhibit many of the key strategies that are needed to lead the DSC. Segmentation, the focus on talent, strategic selection of data and technology innovation, and a focus on cultural alignment are all demonstrated.

The firm's supply chain leadership approach is to find ways of standardizing, applying standards in segments, and gradually building replicable capabilities, all while focusing on customers and innovation.

In the company's leadership development programs, which has been rolling out from a core, centralized academy emphasizes the people component central to enabling digital change at scale.

Required mindsets and culture that the case company felt are key to unlocking transformation include:

1. Customer-centric product innovation with lower barriers to taking risks (a culture that allows for learning from failure)
2. Prioritization and sequencing – the ability to focus on the right thing and sequence them in the right way to create value that aligns with business priorities.
3. Internal process innovation in the way the firms works
4. End-to-end mindset – prioritizing and realigning metrics to support behaviors that benefit the whole, even if your individual metrics are compromised

Digital Supply Chain Case Questions

1. This case company seems to have covered many of the bases needed to achieve transformational performance from the digital supply chain. From the case materials, do you see any potential blind spots?
2. What are some examples of competitive threats that the case firm should be aware of? What kinds of digital supply chain strategies might they be competing with?
3. How do you think this case company finances its digital supply chain improvement projects?
4. How do you think the firm's attempts at centralizing key capabilities, standardizing core processes, and promoting digital mindsets are received by the different, diverse, and fairly independent business units?
5. Are there potential risks inherent in the digital supply chain strategies outlined by this firm? If you do think there are risks, what are they and why do you think they might be causes for concern?
6. Are there global or industry level issues that might turn this complex and elegant set of digital strategies on its head? Will these actions described in the case be enough to offset the challenges of the generic threat and the drying up innovation pipeline?

Summary

- Advancements in IoT, sensors, artificial intelligence, machine learning, robotics, and 3D printing are some of the most potentially disruptive technologies for supply chains. Supply chain leaders cannot afford to have a superficial understanding of these technologies if they are to remain competitive.
- Key strategic goals and objectives for managing technology are as follows: the critical evaluation of new technologies and data sources; the strategic selection of technology; and lastly the deployment of technology in creative, connected, and integrated ways. Technology solutions should unlock hard to replicate business models that customers and consumers benefit from.
- Generative design is an example of a technology that may have transformational impacts on supply chains. With generative design it becomes possible to produce manufactured products that are beyond the capabilities of humans to reproduce.
- Strategically chosen technology pilots should be deployed, along with specific metrics, for measuring business improvement outcomes.
- Technology investments should be aligned to business strategy and not solely the result of unstructured exploration. Persuasive leadership is required to recruit, motive, and engage organizational partners in the boundary spanning collaborative and data sharing required to successfully deploy integrated technologies.

Notes

1 https://support.mapmyfitness.com/hc/en-us/articles/360035381752-UA-Record-Will-No-Longer-Be-Supported Retrieved August 13, 2020.
2 https://www.supertrendsinstitute.com/us/venkat-venkatraman/ Retrieved August 13, 2020.
3 https://www.forbes.com/sites/quora/2017/04/21/what-is-jeff-bezos-day-1-philosophy/#41e980c31052 Retrieved August 13, 2020.
4 https://www.prnewswire.com/news-releases/under-armour-opens-ua-lighthouse-manufacturing-and-design-leadership-center-in-the-brands-hometown-of-baltimore-300291156. Retrieved August 13, 2020.
5 https://www.underarmour.com/en-us/p/running/mens-ua-hovr-infinite-2-running-shoes/3022587.html?start=0&breadCrumbLast=UA%20Connected Retrieved August 13, 2020.

References

Ehrhardt, E., Hutchens, R., & Higgins, S. (2014). *Five steps toward a revitalized pharmaceutical supply chain*. Booz Allen Reprint No. 00094.

Jauhar, S. K., & Pant, M. (2016). Genetic algorithms in supply chain management: A critical analysis of the literature. *Sādhanā, 41*(9), 993–1017. doi:10.1007/s12046-016-0538-z

Kurz, D. (2020). Leading the digital supply chain. In Simmers, C. A. & Anandarajan, M. (Eds.). *The Internet of People, Things and Services: Workplace Transformations*. New York: Routledge.

LeVine, S. (2019). Racing for AI rules. Axios Future. Retrieved July 2019, from https://www.axios.com/newsletters/axios-future-de680fc5-2f6b-4d77-a309-41e242db5202.html

Lohr, S. (2012). The age of big data. *The New York Times*. Retrieved August 11, 2012, from http://www.nytimes.com/2012/02/12/sunday-review/big-datas-impact-in-theworld.html?pagewanted=all.

Lopez, J., & Andrews, W. (2019). *The six strategic design principles for AI applications*. Gartner research note, February 2019. https://www.gartner.com/en/documents/3902315/the-six-strategic-design-principles-for-ai-applications

Majeed, M., & Rupasinghe, T. (2017). *Internet of Things (IoT) embedded future supply chains for industry 4.0: An assessment from an ERP-based fashion apparel and footwear industry. Journal of Supply Chain Management*, 6(1), 25–40.

Michel, R. (2017). The evolution of the digital supply chain. *Logistics Management*, May 23-25, Available at : https://www.logisticsmgmt.com/article/the_evolution_of_the_digital_supply_chain

Paley N. (2017). *Leadership strategies in the age of big data, algorithms, and analytics*. Productivity Press. ProQuest Ebook Central. http://ebookcentral.proquest.com/lib/drexel-ebooks/detail.action?docID=5257684. Created from drexel-ebooks on 2018-07-24 13:23:47."

Walker, M., Andrews, W., & Cearley, D. (2018). *Top 10 strategic technology trends for 2018: AI Foundation*. Gartner research note, March 2018. https://www.gartner.com/en/documents/3865401/top-10-strategic-technology-trends-for-2018-ai-foundatio0

Source: https://www.supertrendsinstitute.com/us/venkat-venkatraman/ Retrieved 8/13/2020

https://www.supertrendsinstitute.com/us/venkat-venkatraman/ Retrieved 8/13/2020

https://www.forbes.com/sites/quora/2017/04/21/what-is-jeff-bezos-day-1-philoso phy/#41e980c31052 Retrieved 8/13/2020

https://www.prnewswire.com/news-releases/under-armour-opens-ua-lighthouse-manufacturing-and-design-leadership-center-in-the-brands-hometown-of-baltimore-300291156.html#:~:text=Under%20Armour%2C%20Inc.&text=The %20UA%20Lighthouse%20will%20be,Under%20Armour%20product%20is %20made.&text=Proven%20processes%20and%20technologies%20created, global%20teammates%20and%20partner%20factories. Retrieved 8/13/2020

7   Understanding and Managing Digital Supply Chain Risks

Moving along the digital supply chain leadership road map introduced in Chapter 4, there is one crucial, and often overlooked, step remaining before we implement and scale new supply chain segments in our businesses. This step is to identify, assess, and manage business performance and compliance risks that are inherent and emerging as a result of our digital supply chain actions. Business risk management is not, of course, a new topic, even as seemingly novel examples of risk emerge in cybersecurity, health and safety, and compliance. New types of risk will always emerge as business, political, regulatory, and world health situations change (Dolgui et al., 2018). A global pandemic, for instance, was not on many business leaders' lists of risks to manage nearing the end of 2019 (Moss, 2020). COVID-19 has now become one of the most disruptive events in modern history, wreaking havoc on lives, economies, and supply chains. The reason the leadership road map includes risk management is not because there are new or increasing risks that have emerged, it is due to the nature of the digital supply chain itself: the complex and interactive nature of business value creation becomes more dependent upon shared activities and outcomes as it becomes more integrated, collaborative, and broader.

Why Is Business Risk Different in Digital Supply Chains?

Consider two figures shared in this book thus far. Figure 3.2 illustrates potential data sources in the supply network and Figure 6.1 shows the end-to-end UnderArmour ArchiTech example. These two figures show the degree of potential increase in data complexity, as well as the interconnectedness of data sharing across supply networks.

Increase in Data Complexity

The digital supply chain relies on large amounts of data from a wide variety of sources, including internally generated and managed data, as well as external data. Customer data, supplier data, third-party logistics firms, not to mention internal transaction system data from supply chain functions, are just a very few examples of the digital information streams flowing in supply chains. Data can be gathered from transactional system data stores, along with identified, curated data made accessible from less structured, but still strategic, sources. Data governance practices should set strategies for how data are identified, accessed, stored, and provisioned for use. Data governance may well include risk and compliance factors in managing enterprise information, but as the number, size, and disparity of data sources increase, so does the risk of being compromised. The digital supply chain may unlock transformational levels of business performance, but to do so requires a higher degree of data sharing, fluidity, and accessibility across networks, value chain partners, and business model actors. It is readily clear that the element of business risk increases significantly as these digitally enabled data models take hold in firms.

Increase in Data Connectedness

Just as the number and volume of data sources increase in the digital supply chain, so too does the degree to which data and information are shared both inside and outside the firm. This sharing can be a conundrum for while our goal in the firm may be to increase supply chain performance by implanting digital supply chain segment designs, doing so may rely on or require data from an increased number of entities or domains. Some data sources which may unlock performance increases, such as access to customer data, are high value and extremely sensitive. High value data sources must be protected from exposure to outside actors, for obvious security reasons, as well as compliance, and competitive threats. While this may be indisputable on some level, it is up to supply chain leaders to ensure that risk management procedures are designed and implemented consistently in the most business-critical areas. Risk management in organizations can quickly become decentralized, misaligned, reactive, and fall out of compliance if left to itself. New, potentially competitively advantaged and connected business models may deliver exciting new business revenues and reach new customers. They will also likely bring new business and compliance risks along with them. Risk management is included in the digital supply chain leadership road map because addressing these new risks may not be second nature as with more traditional business models that rely less on interconnectedness. Until these more connected business models become normalized, supply chain leaders must continue to push for a more proactive risk management culture in their organizations.

The Number and Variety of Business and Compliance Risks Are Increasing

Basic risk management procedures follow some pragmatic steps with the first step being to identify a list of potential risks, a step that was significantly easier before the COVID-19 global pandemic which caught most supply chain leaders by surprise. After identifying the types of risk possible for a given supply chain, the next step is to determine which of the risks identified are more likely. Cyber security risks have become more commonplace in all businesses, and, of course, highly probable in digital supply chains. The final basic step is to determine which risk mitigation steps to follow for the highest impact, most probable risks. Most risk managers do not think it is feasible to develop risk mitigation plans for all risks. It is also not good practice to ignore high probability and high business impact risks. This basic process should be a normal part of digital business segment design. What new business or compliance risks are introduced as a result of serving new customers with supporting data, technologies, partners, or suppliers for the digital supply chain segment being designed and developed? Does this new supply chain design include new partners that have not been used before, such as a component supplier? Does our sourcing team have the proper procedures in place to ensure the new supplier is compliant with key business and regulatory policies? As the supply chain leader, you may need to push for the development of new policies, as well as set the conditions to create a sensible risk management culture in your firm.

Some Common Supply Chain Risks (Moss, 2020)
Business Performance -

- Quality – from your own or supplier off-spec components/finished goods
- On-time Delivery –OTIF targets with your customers
- Price - volatility and scarcity issues
- Credit risks – delayed or missed payments from customers
- Sole source suppliers – concentrated where there are no substitutes or potential for delays
- Product security and counterfeits – IP theft
- Natural disaster – Tsunami, hurricanes, and so forth
- Pandemic – New for 2020
- Political disruption – Trade policy issues

Compliance & Regulatory – vary globally by region and country

- Labor
- Environment – laws, guidelines, and perceptions

- Health and safety – regulations and practical issues (pandemic impacts)
- Human trafficking – child and other exploitative labor (global issue)
- Conflict minerals – e.g., Responsible Minerals Assurance Process (RMAP)
- Corruption – e.g., Foreign Corrupt Practices Act (FCPA)
- Data privacy – e.g., GDPR
- IP & trade secret protection
- Cybersecurity – growing in prevalence and sophistication every day

Some Implications of Managing Supply Chain Risks

This list continues to grow in size and complexity for regional and global firms. Just keeping abreast of the potential compliance and regulatory issues requires time and resources. The implications for supply chain leaders are extensive. Take the issues of human trafficking and conflict minerals compliance. For well-integrated firms, keeping track of labor and production inputs may be within your immediate control. In a more complex value chain, the number and globalization factors for suppliers and other value chain partners increase exponentially. We may have implemented strong controls for our suppliers to qualify them in these issues, but what about their suppliers, or their suppliers' suppliers? Technologies such as Blockchain may offer some promise and show early signs of support for firms' seeking assurance about sourcing compliance (Korpela et al., 2017; Kshetri, 2018). SAP recently announced[1] a service utilizing Blockchain shared ledger technology to help Bumble Bee Foods trace the journey of yellowfin tuna from Indonesia to consumers. The compliance risk in this case is food safety and the use of sustainable sourcing practices. The ramifications of being held responsible or liable for the actions of third parties acting on a firm's behalf is sobering. Assessing risks and the probability of being impacted is critical in order to direct risk management resources to the places where they are most needed to sustain business operations.

Developing a Risk Management Culture

The reality for many firms facing the transition to being more digital in their operations is that they may not currently have an adequate and coordinated risk management function in place. Very often there are disconnects and handoffs, with the HR department handling labor issues, the sales or IT team managing customer data privacy, supply chain sourcing controlling third-party compliance. The digital supply chain leader should seek to build risk management checkpoints in their cross-functional segment design and development efforts. After designing a segment, or just prior to or after a deployment, a coordinated risk management effort is often met with resistance from both internal departments as well as third parties (Duhadway et al., 2018). Proactively introducing risk and compliance professionals into the design process will promote a co-creation mindset, reduce exposure, and potentially dangerous post-implementation mitigation or out of compliance conditions (Moss, 2020).

Developing Risk Management Maturity

How can supply chain leaders develop a sense of where their firm is with respect to risk management and develop a realistic plan based on where they would like to be? Start by self-assessing where your firm is for each supply chain segment. The Digital Supply Chain Institute's risk maturity framework allows leaders to rate themselves against a three-level metric (Digital Supply Chain Institute [DSCI], 2017). Level one is largely reactive risk management, that is, the firm usually waits until there is some evidence of imminent risk before taking action. Level two sees the firm taking steps to understand risks in segments and to develop mitigation plans. Level three is highly data driven and features the firm demonstrating the capability of risk prediction and reduction using integrated information, tools, and processes. As the assessment tool describes this level, the firm uses data analytics to seek patterns in supply chain risks and related negative impacts and adjust our risk management program to reduce or prevent recurrence. The DSCI (2017) maturity assessment describes the following best practices for supply chain leaders managing risks:

- Use data to reduce business performance and compliance risk through predictive analytics
- Place special focus on cybersecurity and data protection
- Strategically segment risks focusing on what to manage and where to selectively excel to gain a competitive advantage

Being Selective in Managing Supply Chain Risks

With the growing number of risks facing firms, it is likely beyond reach to have extensive plans for managing the majority of them (Lu et al., 2019). The first step, as mentioned, is to identify the critical risks that are likely to occur for a given supply chain segment. Then the issue becomes selecting where to focus. Firms could focus on the critical high-risk areas or choose to become excellent in a select number of them. Risk management practice has often promoted the idea that firms may be able to turn certain types of risks into a source of competitive advantage. Credit card firms famously use data analytic techniques to segment their card service portfolios and manage them according to the risk profiles exhibited. This allows these firms to expand their customer bases in certain hard-to-reach segments. By developing more finely tuned analytics capabilities, these firms are able to grow revenues, enhance profitability, and continue to manage risk in a way that has expanded their risk tolerance frontier.

While supply chain leaders may not have business models that reflect the card services industry, they might take a cue from this strategy and reflect on where they could invest in more acute risk management capabilities to enable growth in segments previously out of reach. From a compliance perspective, it is also imperative to reduce the potential negative brand impacts of public perception. Imagine an outdoor clothing and equipment firm being reported as being out of compliance on environmental issues (Moss, 2020) or a luxury brand being accused of child labor violations. These are not simple cost and benefit supply chain decisions; they are essential aspects of protecting a firm's brand reputation.

Case Example

Multinational Conglomerate Manufacturer and Brand Marketer of Building Products and Industrial Chemicals

Industry and Competitive Landscape

This industry includes the manufacture of building materials, home improvement products but does not include construction materials such as forest products and cement. The target customer and consumers can range from professional contractors, to individuals performing home improvements. It is one of the least digitized of industries showing very little in the way of automated business processes, digital connections with consumers, or its own workforce. With many of the industries product segments tied to the construction industry, its sales volumes are quite sensitive to housing starts. A large percentage of products are sold through home improvement retailers such as Lowes and Home Depot. In addition to the building products industry, the case company also manufactures industrial chemicals in bulk for commercial customers. This sector tracks closer to the overall global economic growth and performance.

Organizational Situation

The case company has a wide variety of business sectors, customers, and end users in its portfolio. With its origins as a venerable industrial-oriented manufacture of a wide variety of products, the firm has grown up with minimal efforts at organizational, business unit, or data integration. Rudimentary implementation of Enterprise resource planning systems remained somewhat siloed. There has been minimal effort to manage master data, and a recent project to consolidate procurement commodity data to find and leverage sourcing relationships has been stalled due to incongruities in data sets. Forecasts are critical to planning manufacturing runs, yet the ability to bring in external data sets (such as housing starts) into the process has been slow. Data quality and alignment has been a source of problems for planners and decision makers. Being a high-intensity manufacturing business, process control data from manufacturing assets are extremely important to manage quality and efficiency, yet opportunities for collecting, consolidating, and integrating this data remain untapped. The company sells bulk industrial chemicals to customers that store them in large tank farms adjacent to customer owner manufacturing sites. Historically, customers have managed the inventories of these chemicals and placed replenishment orders with our case company at somewhat unpredictable intervals.

The case company has what might be called a risk averse culture, that is, innovations and changes to existing processes are viewed with caution and are slow to be implemented. Supply chain expertise and technology teams to support them are disbursed throughout the firm by business unit and sometimes by individual product teams.

Leadership Response

The case company supply chain leadership developed remediation strategies for three main focus areas: Data Quality, Technology, and Talent/Organizational Capability.

Data Quality and Integration

This set of workstreams was intended to improve the data governance, quality, and accessibility of data and information from a variety of disparate sources. A solution that would allow for access to disaggregated legacy data, mapping it to a data lake and applying data quality analytics to improve alignment will be critical. Creating a mechanism to provision data to company analyst and data scientists is also needed. A key outcome of the data quality initiatives is to improve forecasting capabilities. Forecast accuracy improvements were viewed to have very high business impact to this firm as surprise orders had the potential to wreak havoc on large batch production schedules.

Technology Efforts

A separate but related effort the firm initiated was to develop and implement strategies for Internet of Things (IoT) sensor-based data, as well as develop and deploy better process control automation. Given the particular type of products this case firm manufactured, supply chain leaders felt that developing capabilities with IoT sensor technology might yield significant digital supply chain performance improvements. Ideas that were floated were as follows:

IoT sensors on bulk chemical freight to keep track of inventory in transit. IoT sensors placed on customer owned bulk chemical storage tanks to monitor inventory levels and calculate usage statistics, also to help in replenishment forecasting and manufacturing runs. Ideas were also floated about improving process control automation to improve manufacturing yields for batch chemical production processes. Waste reduction and the reduction of lead times and fewer changeovers were cited as possible benefits.

Talent and Organizational Efforts

The case firm recognized that it did not have enough talent and capability on hand to activate some of its digital supply chain strategies. Process control automation problems, in particular, seemed to require an ability to solve complex mathematical problems, something beyond the skill sets of the supply chain staff, and even some of the engineers in the firm. The case company began to develop relationships with doctoral programs in local universities and engaged promising PhD mathematics students in joint efforts to share data sources and collaboratively work to solve complex issues. It also began to assign its recruiters certain kinds of supply chain problems through research projects, rather than search for skills, recruiters had defined problems with which to attract and recruit expertise. One of the challenges the firm faced was developing a recruitment strategy that was appealing to highly skilled data scientists. Being an older manufacturing-oriented brand, the firm suffered a disadvantage in recruiting talent compared with its more up to date digital native companies.

For the talent the company did have to work with, agile cross-functional scrum teams were developed that were focused on issues of data integration, as well as decision processes for prioritizing projects for digital automation.

Digital Supply Chain Case Questions

1. What are some of the challenges associated with digital supply chain transformation for business conglomerates?
2. Do you think the firm's legacy organization creates a unique set of challenges in its digital supply chain transformation?
3. What sorts of challenges do you think the firm will encounter as it attempts to implement some of its technology strategies like IoT sensors?

4. How common do you think it is to have a risk averse culture in organizations like the case company? What can be done from a leadership perspective to help change culture and reduce cultural barriers to implementing digital supply chain strategies?
5. Can this firm afford to defer it shift to a more digitally integrated organization?
6. How would you decide where to start in developing digital transformation plans? Do you think the case firm has done a good job of prioritizing its efforts?
7. What about more consumer facing businesses, like home improvement products? How would the case firm go about developing plans for those segments and sectors? Do you think they would be a lot different than efforts required for the industrial chemical division?
8. What are some examples of competitive threats that the case firm should be aware of? What kinds of digital supply chain strategies might they be competing with?
9. How do you think the company's marketing and sales departments differ from those of other industries and markets?
10. Are there potential risks inherent in the digital supply chain strategies outlined by this firm? If you do think there are risks, what are they and why do you think they might be causes for concern?

Summary

- Risk management in the digital supply chain is more critical than ever due to the changing nature of the supply chain itself. A digital supply chain is inherently more complex and data intensive. It is also highly dependent upon shared activities as it becomes more integrated, collaborative, and end-to-end.
- Two factors illustrate the new risk environment for supply chain leaders, an increase in data complexity, and a commensurate increase in data connectedness. Data complexity is the result of the large amounts of data from a wide variety of sources now being utilized to power new business models. Data connectedness is driven by the increasing degree to which data are shared both inside as well as outside the firm.
- In addition to data issues, the number and variety of business and compliance risks are increasing. Business performance risks include quality issues, On-Time-In-Full targets, pricing pressures, credit impacts, supplier dependencies, political disruptions, and now pandemics.
- Compliance and regulatory risks vary by region and include labor issues, environmental, health and safety, human trafficking, data privacy, intellectual property protections, and cyber security.

- To become a more mature risk managed supply chain, leaders should focus on developing their firm's risk management culture, increase their use of data analytics to reduce risks, placing a special focus on cybersecurity and data protection, and becoming more selective in managing specific risks.

Notes

1 https://news.sap.com/2019/03/bumble-bee-foods-sap-create-blockchain-track-fish/

References

Dolgui, A., Ivanov, D., & Sokolov, B. (2018). Ripple effect in the supply chain: an analysis and recent literature. *International Journal of Production Research, Taylor Francis, Leading scholars in Production Research*, 56(1–2), 414–430.

Digital Supply Chain Institute (DSCI). (2017). Digital supply chain transformation guide: Essential metrics [white paper]. *Center for Global Enterprise.* https://www.dscinstitute.org/assets/documents/Digital-Supply-Chain-Transformation-Guide-Essential-Metrics_DSCI_Oct2.pdf

Duhadway, S., Carnovale, S., & Kanna, V. (2018), Organizational communication and individual Behavior: Implications for Supply Chain Risk Management. *Journal of Supply Chain Management*, 54(4), 3–19.

Korpela, K., Hallikas, J., & Dahlberg, T. (2017). Digital supply chain transformation toward blockchain integration. Proceedings of the *50th Hawaii International Conference on System Sciences*, 2017. https://doi.org/10.24251/hicss.2017.506

Kshetri, N. (2018). Blockchain's roles in meeting key supply chain management objectives. *International Journal of Information Management*, 39, 80–89.

Lu, G., Koufteros, X., Talluri, S., & Hult, G. T. (2019). Deployment of supply chain security practices: Antecedents and consequences. *Decision Sciences, Decision Sciences Institute*, 50(3), 459–497.

Moss, C. (2020, July 9). *Risk management in the digital supply chain [Conference presentation]*. Digital Supply Chain Institute. Leading the Digital Supply Chain Program, Zoom Presentation, United States.

8   Becoming an End-to-End Integrated Supply Chain

Leading supply chains is a complex interconnected business as supply chain culture has always been highly focused on efficiency, cost reduction, inventory management, and metrics such as on-time-in-full. Many organizations have even dictated certain percentages of annual cost reduction for operations as a central strategy but finding ways to cut costs without sending product quality into a noticeable decline takes vigilance and creativity. Efficiencies, when found, are often claimed and repurposed for other organizational initiatives, rather than remaining within the supply chain for investment and experimentation. The ability to collaborate with the leaders of other organizational functions to explore ways of integrating is limited. Problems occur and fires have to be put out within your own immediate operations. A head of supply chain for a global pharmaceutical firm was asked in a research interview, "If you could change one thing about your supply chain associates' mindsets, so that if they came in tomorrow and thought about their operations differently, what would it be?" Upon reflection to this seemingly simple question, similar to "Who are your customers?", the Pharmaceutical supply chain executive's answer was that his firm's associates would understand the end-to-end upstream and downstream impacts of their own actions. He went on to elaborate that the current mindset was very focused on "firefighting" problems within the associate's immediate function, even when the problems they were solving were created by upstream actions from other parts of the organization. What the executive described is the leadership behavior of taking a step back to consider why the current issue was created, irrespective of where in the supply chain it may originate, and to take the courageous step of crossing a functional threshold to address problems at their source. Other firms have described the challenge as a business growth issue. For example, a global beverage manufacturer had set the ambitious goal of doubling the size of its business in 10 years. Supply chain leaders were tasked with supporting this level of business growth without a corresponding doubling of supply chain cost. In both examples, better end-to-end integration and collaboration were critical in meeting the business goals of the firm. The key to unlocking this more integrated and enterprise way of working might be called a supply chain leadership mindset, a set of new organizational behaviors that make digital supply chain transformation possible.

The Need for Organizational Learning of Integrator Behaviors

There are critical behaviors needed to facilitate the scaling of digital and supply chain performance transformations. Firms must approach developing the behaviors as an organizational learning challenge requiring intervention (Argyris & Schön, 1978). In our beverage manufacturer example, the firm identified a key set of behavioral enablers allowing for a faster and more impactful deployment of the new systems. The underlying driver of this is that employees should feel empowered and encouraged to act on behalf of the end-to-end organization, rather than acting narrowly within self-interest-driven individual metrics. To realize this goal associates need to develop trust in the alignment of segment plans with the holistic goals of the firm; a belief in the benefits of collaboration and a mindset that allows for functional boundary-spanning behavior.

People Are the Key to Navigating Supply Chain Digital Disruption

Key Dimensions of Digital Supply Chain People Performance

High-performing firms recognize that leadership behaviors are critical to unlocking more integrated supply chain performance. Employee attitudes, beliefs, and actions are magnified under a more digitally integrated supply chain. This next section will outline the key digital supply chain leadership attributes that drive performance.

The Digital Supply Chain Leader

The leadership development profession is not light on theories, concepts, and methods. Collaboration as a strategic objective, for instance, may feel to many as a tired act. The question digital supply chain leaders need to ask is how they can promote meaningful, disciplined collaboration amongst employees. Productive, focused, and disciplined collaboration is a key behavior that allows for more integrated performance improvements across functions and disciplines (Hansen, 2009).

Organizational-Level Strategies and Measures

Supply Chain leaders should look closely at the following areas and evaluate where new demands have surfaced due to digital transformation (Kurz, 2018).

1. Ensure that performance and compensation metrics are aligned or shared within the supply chain (Plan Source, Make, Deliver), as well as cross-functionally with marketing, sales, product development, and finance.

    a. The digital supply chain is highly integrated. Therefore, the talent management practices of the leading firms must reflect this by minimizing information and practice silos.

    b. Recognize that associates in the supply chain cannot visualize all possible benefits of integration and collaboration by themselves. Interventions must be developed to overcome this limitation and the barriers to transparency (Ramanathan et al., 2011).

2. Ensure that supply chain leadership promotes alignment of its own digital strategies with overall corporate strategies.

    a. In the digital supply chain, strategies must align with and serve organizational strategy. New, digitally enhanced business models must surface and be developed in concert with supply chain leaders.

    b. Supply chain leaders must be able to interact in peer-to-peer relationships with a range of senior organizational leaders from all functions.

Individual Attitudes, Beliefs, and Behaviors

In addition to organizational-level leadership characteristics, developing an integrated digital supply chain places demands on a higher level of individual and networked performance. Networked performance is the ability of individuals to raise the performance levels of those around them in the organization. To achieve the objective of greater integration, leaders should be concerned with developing: leadership mindset as an attitude, integrator behaviors, mutual gains approach capabilities, and data-driven problem-solving capabilities.

The Supply Chain Leadership Mindset

When supply chain leaders are confronted with supporting an aggressive organizational growth strategy, they realize that old leadership mindsets cannot create the kind of innovative cultural change needed.

The new mindset reflects a clearer sense of collective leadership responsibility. Reacting to problems within one's own function, while overlooking the upstream causes and downstream impacts of individual actions, would not create a cohesive supply chain to support growth without lockstep increases in cost, complexity, and infrastructure. This distributed, or shared, leadership capability is one that cultivates the spirit that all employees are empowered and encouraged to step across their individually defined task thresholds in pursuit of improved collective performance (Conger & Riggio, 2012; Prokesch, 2010). A supply chain manager with a leadership mindset is not afraid to challenge assumptions about how things are done no matter how established the routine, nor who is managing the process. Supply chain leaders who believe it is their primary role and responsibility to satisfy the firm's customers can make better integrated performance decisions. The leadership mindset represents a shift away from local and individual efficiencies to a broader view of overall effectiveness that balances cost and performance (Kurz, 2018).

Digital Supply Chain Integrators

Leadership programs for global supply chains promote common workforce behaviors that promote and unlock end-to-end supply chain performance (Kurz, 2018). These behaviors concern spanning organizational boundaries, cross-functional disciplined collaboration, and problem-solving by seeking greater organizational outcomes. Firms that can build and expand these behaviors in their workforces will benefit from the competitive advantages offered by the digital supply chain more fully.

The New Digital Supply Chain Integrator Behaviors (Kurz, 2018)

1. Reaching across functional boundaries to seek information and understanding
2. Proactively seeking the prevention of problems at their source, irrespective of the originating function
3. Creating and leading effective boundary spanning problem-solving teams
4. Placing performance of the organization ahead of individual or unit performance, in spite of low organizational support or conflicting metrics
5. Exhibiting leadership that demonstrates and encourages network performance[1]
6. Effectively using influence and negotiating capabilities that seek *mutual gains* (Movius & Susskind, 2009)
7. Building relationships with value chain partners which are collaborative, based on mutual gains, and measured by shared performance metrics (as opposed to lowest cost transactions) (Kurz, 2018)

Developing Digital Supply Chain Leaders

Leading organizations spent more than 169 billion dollars on leadership development in North America alone in 2019 (Training Industry, 2020). The best of these programs are custom-designed to exploit the knowledge of the firm's organizational strategy so that participants can engage in leadership topics to be applied to their own roles in the firm. Participants in these programs should expect to improve their general management skills, and perhaps learn more about their own firm's competitive strengths, weaknesses, and positioning.

What is needed, however, is a leadership development program specifically targeting supply chain functional leaders that is tailored to their unique needs, function, and roles (Kurz, 2018).

The Digital Difference

The argument being made in this chapter is that the digital supply chain will require enhancements in the managements' mindset and attitudes, integration behaviors, and skills to realize its competitive advantages. The changes required are more in the realm of organizational behavioral change guided by intervention than in leadership training. Organizational Behavior interventions have traditionally been limited to corporate communications efforts such as face-to-face workshops or training sessions, town hall meetings, and internal media announcements. An organizational leadership program is needed to drive the digital supply chain behaviors and skills needed to execute a firm's strategy (Kurz, 2018).

In a book chapter entitled *Leading the Digital Supply Chain*, Kurz (2018) suggests the following requirements for program intervention design:

- The ability to scale and reach large numbers of people quickly. Face-to-face training sessions for thousands of global associates are expensive, time consuming, and can be inconsistent in message and delivery. Media-based experiences delivered via the web may overcome this issue.
- Teamwork and collaboration must be supported and encouraged through practice. Individuals viewing media pieces in isolation are unlikely to change their behavior; videos of senior leaders sharing the firm's vision and strategy may help build awareness, but they will not likely change the way people act. The ability to interact with a smaller group of participants as a team is required and these teams must work together online in real-time, as well as asynchronously.
- The experience should be purposefully designed to promote and practice cross-functional supply chain problem-solving. This means

creating and guiding work teams in a structured dialog using a set of action learning tasks and activities that have pace, rhythm, and weekly deadlines for sharing results with a larger cohort. The platform should be a social media learning management tool that can be easily modified to drive weekly supply chain challenges in assigned learning teams. This method connects participants in ways that build participant confidence through experience and practice in cross-functional collaborative problem-solving. Behaviors are more likely to change if participants can experience the power of finding first-hand solutions as a team based on real issues facing their own supply chain.

- The experience should allow for the efficient delivery of core leadership perspectives on the transformation of the supply chain and how it supports organizational strategy. Short, well-edited video clips of senior organizational leaders can be prepared to clarify digital supply chain change imperatives and show how they will help the firm achieve its objectives. All managers and associates should be called upon to take leadership actions to initiate change.
- Guided, paced, smaller cohorts of participants are given scaffolded daily activities to build and sustain knowledge, awareness, and, ultimately, change their feelings and perceptions. E-learning technologies and design approaches abound as the effectiveness of the intervention rest on the quality of the program's design. A traditional eLearning design that mimics compliance and skills-based training modules is unlikely to have the desired behavioral change impact. A set of new design principles that is more strategic, based on adult learning theory, change management theory, and a practical recognition of the constraints of daily work demands, is needed to increase the chances of the intervention's success.

The platform itself is basic, allowing a cohort of supply chain participants to experience the program content together and individually. The experience should integrate media activities such as video clips, readings, and threaded discussions, not unlike most common learning management systems. The main design parameters of the experience should be (Kurz, 2018) as follows:

- Virtual synchronous and asynchronous weekly activities for multiple sets of small (40–50 participant) cohorts.
- Activities, such as read, watch, reflect, and discuss, were designed to take approximately 30–40 minutes per day over four weekdays, followed by an hour-long synchronous event led by a facilitator each week. This cadence of activities continues for eight weeks.
- Each weekly series of activities is followed by a strategic supply chain capability theme focused on practical problem-solving applications at Coca-Cola.

- Each problem-solving team, carefully constructed of diverse and cross-functional participants, is expected to report back on collaborative solutions to integrative supply chain challenges aligned to each theme.

The innovation and opportunity this example provides for digital supply chain leadership is not about learning technology or platforms, but how the design builds integrative mindsets and capabilities.

By bringing participants together to practice integrated supply chain problem-solving for regular intervals over multiple weeks, a collective belief in the power of integrative collaboration has a chance to develop in a sustainable way. Participants demonstrate their abilities by finding solutions to complex problems beyond their individual capacities to solve.

Executive Level Integration – What to Do About It

So far in this chapter we have focused on ideas for building a more integrated mindset for associates in organizations and ideas for developing programs that help develop this capability have been described. Organizational alignment to digital supply chain transformation is necessary to realize the benefits of the strategies and investments in new digital segment designs. Before these plans can be executed, supply chain leaders should develop some alignment among the senior leadership of the firm beyond the supply chain function itself. To change many of the creative new end-to-end business models requires some commitment from other functions across the firm. What can the supply chain leader do to help promote this kind of cross-functional leadership alignment?

The following are a few ideas for how to develop this kind of alignment.

Develop collaboration plans with individual functions
The first idea would be to develop a new kind of collaborative relationship with key functional leaders. The most common example of this is the critical relationship between the supply chain leader and the firm's chief financial officer (CFO) as CFOs think about key metrics for supply chain performance in ways that connect them to a firm's overall performance.

Take a look at the following chart which is a compilation of financial metric charts from several sources (Digital Supply Chain Institute [DSCI], 2017) (Camerinelli (2009), Figure 8.1).

The idea behind this chart is to translate key supply chain metrics into their associated downstream financial impacts. Taking inventory days as an example, described in the chart as a critical component of

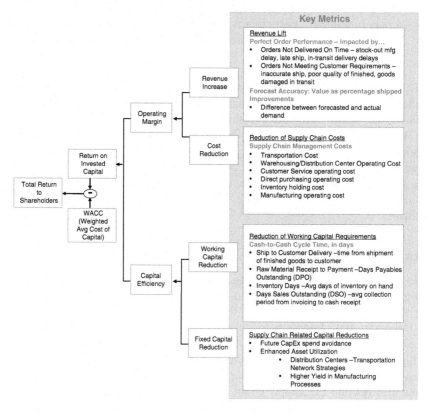

Figure 8.1 Supply Chain Impact Framework.

cash-to-cash cycle time and, therefore, a factor that impacts working capital requirements, we see that improvements in inventory performance will reduce working capital requirements, improve capital efficiency of the firm, and improve return on invested capital (ROIC). This may seem like a basic business concept, but the key is to make sure supply chain leaders are fluent in the ways in which supply chain performance impacts overall financial performance. In critical conversations with the CFO, the supply chain leader should seek to point out how digital actions and potential investments will do more than just improve supply chain performance. It will help to strategically align supply chain actions to enterprise strategy significantly. A common enterprise strategy is to improve the firm's ROIC which benefits firms with external shareholders and the equity analyst community in many ways. Making sure your digital supply chain strategies and actions are aligned and the connections are clearly defined as to how they will support the overall firm's strategy will further the influence and support you receive from senior leadership.

A Note on Metrics and Measurement

To move forward, it is important to look at the metrics currently in use in supply chain. Transformation does not happen overnight, and businesses cannot come to a grinding halt when changing policies and long-standing practices. Existing measures used to assess supply chain performance are, therefore, of paramount importance. For the sake of clarity, we have chosen to describe metrics currently in use today as "traditional" supply chain metrics. These measures represent the role of supply chains centered on facilitating the movement of goods and services but not necessarily the customer-focused or demand-driven ones that are characteristic of digital supply chains. While we recognize the valuable role these traditional measures continue to play in today's supply chain, we firmly believe change must occur for a company to undertake a successful transition to a digital supply chain (DSCI, 2017).

The guiding research questions which were used to shape this investigation were as follows: "What are the supply chain metrics that supply chain leaders care about the most?" and "What are the supply chain performance metrics that are 'universal' in practice across industries and organizations?" In *The Hierarchy of Supply Chain Metrics,* Debra Hofman wrote that the key is to focus on the few critical metrics that really matter. She discusses the ones that provide the most balanced view of end-to-end supply chain performance, and that allow companies to see clearly how they're doing and why, and where they're making trade-offs (Hofman, 2004). These critical metrics and supply chain metrics will be deeply impacted by the digital supply chain. It is important to consider how a firm's digital actions and initiatives will ultimately improve its performance as measured by these key traditional metrics. Examples of possible new digital supply chain metrics can be found in the Appendix. The digital metrics should measure key activities to drive digital supply chain performance improvement. They do not replace traditional metrics but are potential new measures to help guide organizational change (DSCI, 2017).

Digital Supply Chain Strategy Development

Developing individual relationships with senior functional executives is a crucial action. Bringing functional leaders together to align on enterprise digital supply chain strategy is another way to build consensus, support, and jumpstart the broader transformation process. A focused workshop, bringing together key top decision makers from a cross-section of organizational functions, is necessary to understand and identify digital opportunities and to decide on broader digital supply chain actions that may impact business models. Strategic transformation in organizations cannot be accomplished in one swift stroke. The cross-functional interdependences, the shift in mindsets, and decisions about processes and investments require a thoughtful selection of principals starting with a senior-level executive sponsor and cascading to senior functional leaders and their delegates. The executive sponsor of the transformation should, at the very least, be the senior leader of the organization. This sponsor may then delegate a digital supply chain transformation leader to manage the process and be accountable for strategy implementation. For the proposed transformation workshop to be effective, the organization should recruit a transformation steering team that includes senior-level representation from firm-level functions, such as finance, sales, marketing, product development, IT, HR, and supply chain. The members of this steering team, led by the executive sponsor, are the best participants in a transformation workshop. Having key cross-functional leaders present in the workshop allows for the creation of consensus-built actionable strategies.

The workshop team will facilitate an introductory dialog utilizing data about the firm's current level of transformation maturity. Once a baseline understanding of the current performance levels of your firm has been established, each key digital supply chain segment is explored for strategies and actions that can be pressure-tested and deployed in the near term. The workshop outcome will be a deployable digital supply chain action plan tailored to your firm with alignment and support from your key organizational stakeholders. The workshop objectives should be to:

- Understand your firm's current-state digital supply chain maturity
- Develop a process of evaluating performance gaps and improvement opportunities in digital supply chain
- Understand and develop cross-functional actions to overcome the issues, challenges, and potential barriers inherent in digital supply chain transformation
- Improve your firm's speed in implementing critical digital supply chain strategies and actions that will provide immediate performance returns
- Appoint a project leader reporting to the executive sponsor (DSCI, 2017)

Convening a senior executive working group to review supply chain strategies will not be easy and will take a convincing business case for changes to be made as they are linked to the firm's strategy. Planning digital transformation as a campaign focused on targeted segments and developmental horizons is the right leadership approach.

Case Example

*Case: Multinational Manufacturer, Brand Marketer, and
Director Retailor of Computer Hardware*

Industry and Competitive Landscape

The computer hardware market is segmented into several major categories, such as large-scale servers, intended for high volume and high-speed business processing, as well as a wide range of consumer devices. Channels are high end business consulting type contract sales, direct to consumer, as well as big box retail customers like BestBuy. Many consumer-oriented computer technology producers have been increasingly moving to diversify into software and entertainment categories, as well as direct-to-consumer custom configured made-to -order products. The industry is fast moving, and as it has roots in the digital revolution in Silicon Valley, has a digital native culture in many of its well-known firms. While some of the younger technology firms have the advantage of being able to build business models from the ground up with digital, data-driven processes, there are some, more venerable firms that grew to maturity in an earlier era, just before many of the hyper-connected aspects of the integrated digital marketplace were more firmly established. Our case firm is of this latter category, a computing industry veteran, a brand who has been instrumental in shaping technology product supply chain strategies for decades, but now finds itself being challenged by technology start-ups without the weight of legacy processes, systems, and data.

Organizational Situation

The case company is well educated in all thing digital. Its level of maturity in the goals, objectives, and strategies needed to remain competitive in a technologically sophisticated market was high. It has a clear understanding of the strategy, talent needs, the need for transparency of information, and the need for advanced analytics, artificial intelligence, and machine learning. It has a transformation vision that will emphasize scale and agility, as well as cross-functional problem-solving aligned with digital objectives. In short, the case firm has everything it needs, including dedicated resources, and senior leadership support that should enable a smooth transition to a fully digital business. Yet even with all of these advantages, the firm struggles to achieve the levels of performance it envisions. It hasn't yet realized its digital potential. The reason, supply chain leadership believes is hampering transformation, is the firm's challenges in building an integrated enterprise data model. Building an enterprise-wide digital business data architecture, one that is aligned to the company vision, is more than just a project. It is a large-scale endeavor of its own, one involving organizational effort, and a significant reimagining of how the company does business.

Leadership Response

One lesson from this case is that even the firms who seemingly have many advantages in the transition to a mode digital supply chain and business encounter leadership challenges in doing so, especially if they have large-scale global operations that have grown up under different rules, business models, and disparate data governance approaches. Many firms have told the same story, that is start with data governance, and start early. It is the key to being able to take advantage of digital analytics and processes down the road. Gaining traction in managing data for the enterprise is much harder than it sounds. The following outlines some of the steps the case company has taken to gain control over its key digital business enabler, data.

The enterprise digital transformation leaders decided to tackle this daunting task of building an enterprise data architecture populated with high-quality data aligned to the company needs by designing and building a data lake. The data that would populate the lake needed to be timely, and trustworthy. It requires data lake teams charged with identifying data sources, developing data models that align with the architecture of the lake, that would also run the projects and roadmaps needed. The teams would supplement themselves with internal and at times external programming expertise needed to accomplish the complex tasks of curating data through aligning disparate systems, developing schemas, identifying where there were missing data sources, coding data quality improvement algorithms, and setting and measuring compliance with business specific compliance targets.

The teams were charged with going about their tasks in an agile development manner of self-organization and collaboration keeping the end user in mind as they set goals and solved supply chain problems.

The People and Leadership Component

The transformation leadership team paid close attention to the organizational behavior component of the data lake working teams. They provided the teams with digital working tools that allowed them to overcome information sharing and collaboration barriers. They were provided training in the tools, as well as modules designed to increase program engagement and motivation. The teams were carefully designed to represent current, as well as future collaborative roles. Care was taken to ensure that teams were not chosen only for their skills and toolset experience, but how they might interact and build trust. The transformation leadership realized that building a data lake is one thing. Building a data lake that the digital workforce and decision makers across the enterprise would value, trust, and use in making business decisions is another. The composition of the work teams served not only to carry out the tasks at hand but also to help overcome any resistance through promoting and disseminating the veracity of the effort and anticipate the benefits of its completion.

The transformation leadership team invested heavily in the data lake program. When asked why this program received so much attention, the leadership team responded that the effort required to transform the company to a high-performance digital supply chain would be cut in half with the implementation of the fully operational enterprise data lake.

Digital Supply Chain Case Questions

1. What are some the issues with implementing large-scale data governance and provisioning programs?
2. Do you agree with the transformation leadership team that the data lake program was the starting point for and the key enabler of all things digital in the supply chain?
3. Is there anything you might do differently in developing a strategic approach for enabling the case company to take advantage of the benefits of the digital supply chain?
4. Did the case company narrative include anything about customers and consumers of the company's products? Is the transformation approach customer centric?
5. Do you think that the digital supply chain means different things for different companies depending on what industry they are in, what segments they serve, what channels they address, and how mature they are in key attributes?
6. Do you think the firm's legacy organization creates a unique set of challenges in its digital supply chain transformation?
7. Why do you think data lake users might not trust the data they are using that is provided to them? What can the program team do to improve the level of trust in the data?
8. Are there potential risks inherent in the digital supply chain strategies outlined by this firm? If you do think there are risks, what are they and why do you think they might be causes for concern?

Summary

- High-performing firms recognize that leadership behaviors are critical to unlocking more integrated supply chain performance.

Employee attitudes, beliefs, and actions are magnified under a more digitally integrated supply chain.

- Ensure that performance and compensation metrics are aligned or shared within the supply chain functions, as well as cross-functionally with marketing, sales, product development, and finance.
- Ensure that supply chain leadership promotes alignment of its own digital strategies with overall corporate strategies.
- Leadership programs for global supply chains promote common workforce behaviors that promote and unlock end-to-end supply chain performance. The chapter summarizes some of these key behaviors and refers to them as integrator behaviors.
- Integrator behaviors are as follows:

  o Reaching across functional boundaries to seek information and understanding
  o Proactively seeking the prevention of problems at their source, irrespective of the originating function
  o Creating and leading effective boundary spanning problem-solving teams
  o Placing performance of the organization ahead of individual or unit performance, in spite of low organizational support or conflicting metrics
  o Exhibiting leadership that demonstrates and encourages network performance
  o Effectively using influence and negotiating capabilities that seek *mutual gains*
  o Building relationships with value chain partners which are collaborative, based on mutual gains, and measured by shared performance metrics (as opposed to lowest cost transactions)

- Supply chain leadership development programs must specifically target supply chain functional leaders that are tailored to their unique needs, function, and roles
- Executive level integration that focuses on organizational alignment to digital supply chain transformation is needed to promote cross functional performance. Supply chain leaders should develop collaboration plans with individual corporate functions, like finance, in order to gain support for investments in digital.
- The Supply Chain Impact Framework is designed to help supply chain leaders think through how specific digital actions might trickle down to key firm financial metrics that are in the realm of finance. Making sure your digital supply chain strategies and actions are aligned and the connections are clearly defined as to how they will

support the overall firm's strategy will further the influence and support you receive from senior leadership.

- Planning digital transformation as a campaign focused on targeted segments and developmental horizons is a winning leadership approach.

Notes

1 Network performance is the behavior of taking action to raise the performance levels of those around you. It goes beyond individual task performance (CEB, 2014)

References

Argyris, C., & Schön, D. (1978). *Organizational learning: A theory of action perspective*. Reading, MA: Addison Wesley.

Camerinelli, E. (2009). *Measuring the value of the supply chain: Linking financial performance and supply chain decisions*. Routledge.

CEB. (2014). *The rise of the network leader. Reframing leadership in the new work environment*. The Corporate Executive Board Company. https://www.cebglobal.com/content/dam/cebglobal/us/EN/top-insights/executive-guidance/pdfs/eg2014ann-rise-of-network-leader.pdf.

Conger, J. A., & Riggio, R. E. (2012). *The practice of leadership: Developing the next generation of leaders*. Wiley.

Digital Supply Chain Institute (DSCI). (2017). Digital supply chain transformation guide: Essential metrics [white paper]. *Center for Global Enterprise*. https://www.dscinstitute.org/assets/documents/Digital-Supply-Chain-Transformation-Guide-Essential-Metrics_DSCI_Oct2.pdf

Hansen, M. T. (2009). *Collaboration: How leaders avoid the traps, create unity, and reap big results*. Boston: Harvard Business Press.

Hofman, D. (2004). *The hierarchy of supply chain metrics: Diagnosing your supply chain health*. AMR Research Report.

Kurz, D. (2018). Leading the digital supply chain. In C. A. Simmers & M. Anandarajan (Eds.), *The Internet of people, things and services: Workplace transformations* (pp. 243–257). London, England: Routledge.

Movius, H., & Susskind, L. (2009). *Built to win: Creating a world-class negotiating organization*. Boston, MA: Harvard Business Press.

Prokesch, S. (2010). *The sustainable supply chain*. Brighton, MA: Harvard Business Review.

Ramanathan, U., Subramanian, N., & Gunasekaran, A. (2011). Supply chain collaboration performance metrics: a conceptual framework. *Benchmarking: An International Journal, 18*(6), 856–872.

Trainingindustry.com. (2020). Size of the training industry. https://trainingindustry.com/wiki/outsourcing/size-of-training-industry/

9 Leading and Developing a Transformation Action Plan

Current and Ongoing Supply Chain Leadership Challenges

The COVID-19 Shock

In the early months of 2020, the global disruption of COVID-19 on the world's economies and individual welfare became apparent. At the time of this writing, in late summer 2020, there is still much to be learned about the pandemic, including when, or if, it will be resolved, and the long-term effects it will have on business and people. From a supply chain leadership perspective, it may be helpful to reflect on what we do know and what the most likely impacts will be for businesses.

Supply chains are coordinated networks of the efforts to deliver the right quantities of products and services customer want and need when they demand them. Each supply chain and segment is different with certain supply chains having proven to be fairly resilient during this current shock, such as types of food supply, while other supply chains have shown signs of strain or having reached a breaking point, as with medical supplies. One key issue supply chain leaders have worked on, which has become even more important during the COVID-19 pandemic, is visibility into supply networks. Firms need to improve their ability to know, at any time, where their items are, together with inputs needed for production, and where their inventories are located to determine what exactly needs to be produced and transported to where they are needed in time. Visibility into raw materials, finished goods, and inventories requires the timely tracking of information, something the digital supply chain (DSC) is highly capable of doing, which, in turn, requires upgrade design, development, and deployment to be realized.

COVID-19 has created, and in some cases revealed, some dramatic problems with existing supply chains. Demand Forecasting models do not take into consideration dramatic pandemic-related disruptions. In normal times, supply chains focus on staying low cost, steady, and lean to deliver just the right amount to satisfy demand, but little or no more.

Those models are immediately broken when a huge disruption takes place and supply chain leaders have to react quickly. The best supply chains have scenarios planned for disruptions and networks in place that can continue when certain nodes, such as China-sourced manufacturing, are disengaged (Allen, 2019). Disruption scenarios are not the same as forecasts, but forecast models may need to be changed out to account for new realities during a disruption and better firms have plans in place for such unexpected events. Lessons are often learned hard as most firms did not have a pandemic scenario in place when COVID-19 struck.

This is an example of how spikes in customer demand, and some extraordinary behaviors, can overwhelm inventories, safety stocks, and even production capacity. Going the other way, once things are back to "normal" creates its own set of problems. The Bullwhip effect in supply chain, a basic reaction to a short-term spike of overproduction, can result in excess inventories of certain products. Years of operating the supply chain as lean as possible with razor-thin levels of safety stocks may need to change. One longer-term result of the pandemic is that holding more inventories of critical components or goods will become more acceptable and standard practice.

The well-publicized case of the shortages of medical supplies and personal protective equipment was disturbing to witness as it unfolded. Was it a supply chain issue, a preparedness issue, or a visibility of supply issue? We do know that it has proven difficult to obtain clear information about inventories, demand, production capacity, and logistics. It is a perfect example of how global and integrated supply chains have become. As a result, investing in digital technologies, such as Control Tower, to improve visibility across the networks is becoming attractive to more firms given the way deficiencies have been exposed by the pandemic.

In the long run we will see more investment in supply networks that are more resilient, can balance global and domestic sourcing and capacity, and have an increased tolerance for investments in higher levels of inventories for items. Investors and senior leadership teams may have to tolerate a more balanced set of measures for firm performance. Business is no longer about just low cost and profits. As risk, safety, and health are crucial elements to firms, investors should do more to recognize and tolerate these factors and reward firms who prove they can perform in balanced ways.

Some Longer-Term Changes to Supply Chains

One area where longer-term disruptive impacts are likely is in the workforce. For supply chain and other business leaders, firms which had a head start in establishing a more digitally enabled workforce, such as allowing workers to work from their homes without losing huge amounts of productivity and access, have been able to survive the disruption better than those which had been putting off digital workforce and relying more on face-to-face interactions to make and deliver products (Meyer, 2017).

Automation is another example. Firms using robotics and more machine-based logistics have fared better than those caught in traditional business models. Prior to COVID-19, investing in digitalization was considered optional, today it has become essential to operational survival in several areas. Firms are now awakening to the need to change business models, and the supply chains that support them, to become more automated and provide fewer friction points without face-to-face human contact (Sanders & Swink, 2019).

Starbucks recently announced the closure of up to 400 company-owned locations over the next 18 months while speeding up the expansion of "convenience-led formats" such as curbside pickup, drive-thru, and mobile-only pickup locations, an example of how firms are adapting to new business models in the wake of this disruption. Firms waiting or refusing to change may find themselves a victim of the next event.

The Hidden Upside – Change May Now Be Possible

As a firm you can take advantage of this disruption. Now is the time to take advantage of technology, data, and automation to set up a more DSC. Supply chains have always been under extreme pressure to produce results with as little cost as possible and when a supply chain produces cost savings, the money is expected to be returned to the firm for redistribution elsewhere, not necessarily back in the supply chain. Quarterly earnings expectations are now wildly off for many companies offering leaders the chance to reset expectations while making changes that would, in ordinary circumstances, appear radical. Firms which can afford to make these changes today may find themselves in a stronger position going forward.

Developing Action Plans for DSC Transformation

If you have arrived at this point by following the DSC leadership roadmap, you may have reached the point where it is necessary to coordinate things better. Our guideposts, steps, questions, and strategy horizons are all useful in formulating transformation actions and plans, but the remaining challenge is how to consolidate the key actions into a coherent and implementable action plan. DSC actions plans are unique to individual leaders, as well as to their organizations, functions, and departments. Starting points will be different, as will technical capabilities, degrees of strategic alignment across functions, and senior

ACTION PLAN

In the table below, write the specific actions you intend to take and the timeframe for taking action. Keep in mind that you may need to adapt things you learned in the course to the specific context of your work environment. It's okay to be a little conservative with your planning but do your best to set deadlines and stick to them.

As you develop action items, be sure to think of yourself in your actual job setting, implementing the activity you have described.

If you have an idea of when you will be able to begin implementing the action items, make a note of it. Three categories can be chosen: 1) within 2 months of completing the program, 2) after two months, or 3) as it arises (you do not know when the opportunity to try this action will occur.)

Action Items	Start to implement Action Plan (check if known)		
I plan to:	Within 2 months	After 2 months	As the opportunity arises

Figure 9.1 A Sample Digital Supply Chain Action Planning Template.

leadership support (Fitzgerald et al., 2014). Action planning will be most useful when it focuses on the core dimensions of segment and time horizon. A useful action plan will resemble "horizon one actions for the eastern US big box retail customer distribution centers." Individual customers within this segment will have their own strategic choices to make and execute as well. Behind the scenes, this segment will have been selected because of its strategic importance to the firm in terms of revenue, profitability, or competitive threat. Once selected, the action plans should follow the iterative development of optimal segment design, data analytic insights, pilot planning and testing, and implementation of digital improvements (Goknur & Guner, 2019). Establishing and monitoring performance metrics, both traditional and digital, should be defined and mechanisms for gathering, calculating, and reporting should be put in place (Figure 9.1).

In developing action plans, committing collectively to implementation deadlines is extremely helpful. When we run DSC leadership programs for executives, we ask participants to complete an action planning template that looks like the following:

This template is to help leaders develop a clear set of actions linked to broader strategic vision. Initial actions may be modest, but they will contribute or start the firm down the path toward significant improvements. A second reason for the template is to socialize the actions for successful projects gain visibility and collective support. One large pharmaceutical firm created a name for its process improvement projects that was well-established and understood as part of the organizational culture. Their supply chain leaders reframed several of the digital transformation actions utilizing the terms of the established processes. The company found that it could actually improve organizational support and buy-in for the transformation projects by not identifying them as something radical or different but as part of normal business improvement activities. The outcomes of the project were completely aligned to the digital transformation horizon plans and were being incrementally accomplished using existing organizational support.

This strategy may also work well when socializing action plans with functions outside of immediate control but where support or integrative execution actions are needed. Large-scale transformation language being used to describe efforts may meet with internal organizational resistance. A savvier way to approach building support from the organization may be to frame initiatives in terms that are more easily understood and comfortable to outside functions (Michel, 2018).

Nevertheless, supply chain leaders should anticipate barriers or challenges as they develop action plans as it is unrealistic to expect any business process, or technology changes required to execute on a segment design, to be welcomed and embraced without some resistance. Our advice is to build these barriers and challenges into the plans themselves and to identify, in advance, what can be done to overcome the challenges and whom you may be able to enlist to help as much as possible. Finally, it is good practice to think in terms of longer-term strategic goals when setting actions. It is wise to remain flexible and anticipate that you may not be able to obtain the ideal piece of data, skillset, or technology you would like for your initial segment design. Being agile and resilient are two terms that are normal operating procedures for supply chain leaders and their teams.

The DSC Maturity Model for Leadership Actions

Here are some key principles to keep in mind as you embark on developing your particular set of digital business actions. First of all, your firm is not alone in this struggle to change and transform. The challenges you are facing are similar to the ones facing your competitors. Digital innovation is happening at an increasingly rapid pace and keeping up is not optional. There are risks to taking digital actions just as there are risks to inaction. In reviewing a three-horizon model for transformational business actions, the critical first step is to develop a strategy and begin the journey. The next steps in the growth horizon are to stay focused on the goals of creating hard-to-replicate integrated capabilities and to enable new business models that allow for the capture of previously inaccessible revenues. Our horizon three goals are to realize the strategic promise of the DSC and bring us full circle back to our premise

Business Models Maturity Assessment

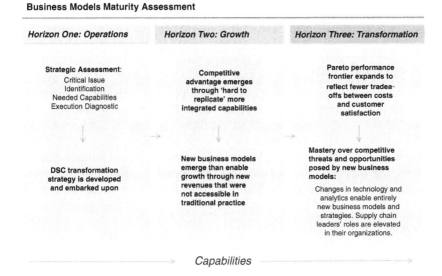

Figure 9.2 DSC Maturity Model for Leadership Actions.

in Chapter 3 by expanding in-text pareto performance to a level reflecting fewer trade-offs between costs and customer satisfaction. By achieving mastery over competitive threats while opening up your firm to new business opportunities, the role of the supply chain leader is ripe for elevation. The supply chain leader who transforms into a DSC leader elevates their role and that of the supply chain in the success of an organization.

Figure 9.2 illustrates the leadership transformation efforts needed to change the organization from a traditional supply chain to a DSC across key focus areas. The central idea being that operational actions needed to deliver performance in the traditional environment are not sufficient for digital business. DSC leaders will need to shift their focus to become more integrated, cross-functional, and technologically sophisticated. The following are some key transformational drivers for each area.

Leadership Focus

The leadership focus for the traditional supply chain has been established for decades. Traditional internal metrics such as perfect order performance, days inventory, transportation costs, and forecast accuracy are the main drivers for everyday operational decision-making and leadership actions. Transformational leadership requires rethinking selected current operations and allowing vision and strategy, informed by priorities, to be unconstrained by current operations. While not a blank slate, the creative use of insights, technology, and business modeling will ideally bring about top- and bottom-line business performance improvements that expand beyond the internal supply chain function.

Operational Focus

The traditional operational focus of the supply chain leader is narrowly on order fulfillment while managing costs. The leadership mindset shift needed for operations is more of a cultural change to support supply chain as a set of processes that are a source of competitive advantage for the firm. By driving and implementing new sensing and stimulation actions, the supply chain function will play a more central role in driving customer satisfaction which means shifting away from order fulfillment.

People Focus

In the traditional supply chain organization, the performance of associates is measured by how well they deliver on their functional metrics and goals. Planners are measured on forecast accuracy, sourcing professionals on the lowest cost for inputs to production acquired, manufacturing leaders on reducing waste, and delivery leaders on the cost of transportation networks. In the DSC, a more integrated view of the end-to-end supply chain requires that leaders reward and measure enterprise performance. Information sharing, incentivized by customer experience metrics rather than siloed functional measures, becomes the new organizational culture (Saenz & Cottrill, 2019). The key in this focus area is to reduce the amount of conflict between functions, such as sourcing being measured based on the lowest cost of raw materials as input and production conflicting with manufacturing quality standards. Another common example is transportation networks being developed based on the lowest levels of inventory and delivery which cause stock-outs and possible delays in meeting customer expectations. The DSC reduces information latency, improves visibility, and allows for more integrated decision-making across functions (Houston et al., 2012). Leaders will need to make this happen because this kind of organizational change will not happen on its own (Wieland et al., 2016).

Technology Focus

Finally, leaders need to focus on the sophisticated use of technology that enables new business value to be unlocked, rather than simply digitizing existing processes. Finding the sources of slow or manual processes or making decisions based on cultural norms rather than data are essential. Resisting the temptation to invest in technologies that provide marginal performance improvement and identifying the sources of strategic value

Table 9.1 Traditional vs. Digital Leadership Behaviors

Focus Areas	The Traditional Supply Chain	Digital Supply Chain Transformational Leadership	The Digital Supply Chain
Leadership Focus	Manage to traditional metrics. Strategies target internal SC performance	Vision and strategy formed by digital unconstrained by current operations	Supply Chain integrated into business strategy driving top line and bottom line performance improvements
Operational Focus	Perfect order targets met while inventory levels managed and balanced	Integrated vision; supply chain as a source of competitive advantage, new digital processes and business models,	Supply Chain helps drive customer satisfaction and revenue increases through sensing and stimulation actions
People Focus	Individual functional performance measures; Plan, Source, Make, Deliver	Sponsorship of organizational behaviors interventions and rewards. Digital Talent Strategy development and execution	Cross-functional collaboration that improves internal and external enterprise performance. Digital savvy workforce
Technology Focus	Forecast accuracy– manual processes	Strategic investment in digital supply chain technologies	Sophisticated use of IoT, sensors, data, analytics, artificial intelligence and machine learning

instead is key. In all of these dimensions the cultural barriers to implementing change and realizing the benefits of actions and investments are as significant, or maybe even more significant, as technological complexity. Overcoming these barriers is one of the most important attributes of the DSC leader (Table 9.1).

The Role of the Chief Supply Chain Officer

This book has taken leadership focus on the transformation of the supply chain to a more integrated digital business. Supply chain leaders are faced with an environment not unlike the information technology leaders from a decade ago. In the decade following the turn of the millennium, digital business, lead largely by digital native companies, such as Amazon, established many of what have become the rules of modern business. As traditional firms struggled to adapt and adjust to the new environment, the role of technologists came to the forefront in many organizations. Technology, now viewed as the key to unlocking new business processes, moved away from being simply an organizational service function, to becoming integrated into business strategy. This transition is largely complete in most firms. The Chief Technology Officer (CTO) now occupies a strategic c-suite role alongside the serious leadership of the firm and helps guide strategy and make decisions about technology that places the firm at a competitive advantage. It is as much externally facing as it is internal. It is expected to help the firm unlock value and innovate. It is expected to be proactive and lead the firm to new sources of customer satisfaction and delight. In a similar fashion, the role of the supply chain leader is now in the same position as that of the CTO a decade ago. To truly lead the supply chain in the world of digital business, firms will need the same kind of innovation mindset. Chief operating officers and DSC leaders will need to be proactive and find new ways to go beyond traditional fulfillment. Business models that integrate technology, as well as operations, require a leader who is comfortable at a strategic level with both. This is the new Chief Supply Chain Officer. It is a set of capabilities, as well as a mindset. It is a journey and a destination for just about every firm on the planet. The challenge will undoubtedly open up supply chain leadership to a new central role as a driver of brand value.

Summary

- Supply chains are coordinated networks that deliver the right quantities of products and services customer want and need when they demand them. COVID-19 has created, and in some cases revealed, some dramatic problems with existing supply chains. Demand forecasting models do not take into consideration dramatic disruptions, such as pandemics.
- In the long run we will see more investment in supply networks that are more resilient, can balance global and domestic sourcing and capacity, and have an increased tolerance for investments in higher levels of inventories for some items. Investors and senior leadership teams may have to tolerate a more balanced set of measures for firm performance.
- Prior to COVID-19, investing in digitalization was considered optional, today it has become essential to operational survival in several areas. As a firm you can take advantage of this ongoing disruption. Now is the time to take advantage of technology, data, and automation to create a more DSC.
- DSC action plans are unique to individual leaders, as well as to their organizations, functions, and departments. Establishing and monitoring performance metrics, both traditional and digital,

should be defined, and mechanisms for gathering, calculating, and reporting should be put in place.

• Supply chain leaders should anticipate barriers or challenges as they develop action plans as it is unrealistic to expect any business process, or technology changes to be welcomed and embraced without some resistance.

• To truly lead the supply chain in the world of digital business, firms will need an innovation mindset. The emerging and enhanced role of Chief Supply Chain Officer will emerge as central figures in driving brand value.

References

Allen, G. (February, 2019). *Understanding China's AI strategy: Clues to Chinese strategic thinking on artificial intelligence and national security.* Washington, DC: Center for a New American Security.

Fitzgerald, M., Kruschwitz, N., Bonnet, D., & Welch, M. (2014). *Embracing digital technology: A new strategic imperative. Findings from the 2013 digital transformation global executive study and research project by MIT Sloan Management Review & Capgemini Consulting (Research Report 2013).* MIT Sloan Management Review, Cambridge, MA, Massachusetts Institute of Technology, pp. 1–12.

Goknur, A. A., & Guner, G. (2019). Strategic management perspectives on supply chain. *Management Review Quarterly.* Advance online publication. https://doi.org/10.1007/s11301-019-00165-6

Gunasekaran, A., Papadopoulos, T., Dubey, R., Wamba, S. F., Childe, S. J., Hazen, B., & Akter, S. (2017). Big data and predictive analytics for supply chain and organizational performance. *Journal of Business Research, 70,* 308–317.

Houston, P., Turner, M. D., Miller, J., & Thelen, B. (2012). Supply management at a crossroads lessons for success in turbulent times. *Booz & Company Perspective, 1–21,* 9.

Meyer, M. (July/August, 2017). *The supply chain workforce of the future. Supply Chain Management Review,* 18–20.

Michel, R. (May, 2018). *Your path to the digital supply chain. Logistics Management Review.*

Saenz, M. J., & Cottrill, K. (January, 2019). *Navigating the road to digital supply chain transformation. Supply Chain Management Review,* 6.

Sanders, N., & Swink, M. (January, 2019). *Digital supply chain transformation: Visualizing the possibilities. Supply Chain Management Review,* 30–34.

Wieland, A., Handfield, R., & Durach, C. (2016). Mapping the landscape of future research themes in supply chain management. *Journal of Business Logistics, 37*(3), 205–212

10 The Supply Chain Leadership Mindset

In this closing chapter, we cast our gaze across numerous case examples and experiences in working with supply chain organizations to explore common current challenges, how firms are responding to these challenges, and then determining solutions leaders will need. Having studied dozens of firms in different industries to uncover patterns of obstacles facing firms and identify promising digital strategies and actions, we categorically focus on what real companies are doing and experiencing. This book has laid out frameworks, tools, concepts, and guides to assist supply chain leaders in practice. These tools and strategies are not based on theory alone. Instead, we pinpoint key challenges and actions from actual problems companies are facing. The findings of this cross-company analysis were striking as there are numerous common challenges confronting many companies, irrespective of industry, markets, or maturity and it is not surprising that many of the common challenges are rooted in the legacies of firms. Digital native companies, those that have grown from their beginnings as customer and data-driven operations, seem to have the advantage over traditional firms seeking to evolve as issues centered around data, culture, change management, business models, metrics, and performance look distinctly different for companies that grew to maturity prior to the more integrated digital landscape we currently inhabit. The following section will look at common themes facing traditional firms seeking to transform to more digital operations and each theme will outline common challenges, noteworthy actions being taken to meet them, and, finally, share some open issues requiring further attention. The themes also share one overarching common thread which is the need for digital leadership approaches.

Theme One: External Forces Requiring Change Leadership

In speaking to many firms across a wide range of industries, it is clear that all are dealing with significant pressures from market forces requiring business responses. Changes in consumer preferences, including some dramatic and lasting cases, have forced some firms to adapt their supply chains to shift to new, more innovative products and away from more traditional products. The changes could be in the form of lifestyle changes, such as health and wellness, or they may be in the form of channel preferences, such as shifts away from retail bricks and mortar, to e-commerce and direct. Competitive entrants to markets are a constant threat which, in most cases, requires an integrated response. To make matters even more difficult, regulatory, public health, and trade policy issues are wreaking havoc on companies, strategies, and supply chains.

These external forces have manifested themselves in some common ways within organizations with the subsequent reaction to these external threats appearing as an appeal to become more agile in a firm's operations. There is a clear need for cultural changes that are less risk averse, more agile, and capable of balancing competing needs around efficiency, product quality, and safety. Another ubiquitous concern for firms regards the need for increases in innovation culture: not simply product or process innovation, but a deep-rooted mindset to drive innovative problem-solving.

Theme One: External Forces and What Firms Are Doing About It

One highly popular approach to support the demand for more agile change is to designate specific teams to focus on strategic change initiatives. Examples of these teams include: digital supply chain transformation teams, teams focused on enterprise data issues, teams charged with driving end-to-end processes, forecast and demand planning teams, and process innovation teams. The team member selection process is often purposeful and, at times, cross-functional in composition. The teams themselves have supply chain executive charters, budgets, and occasional access to cross-functional supply chain data. Designating teams is just the first step, though firms do seem to recognize that adopting a business-as-usual approach reliant upon intact functional teams to address significant market force changes is not adequate.

Theme One: External Forces and What Still Needs To Be Done

We know that much remains to be accomplished in the majority of traditional firms. Task forces may have been identified, initiatives may have been launched, but the critical task of building internal support for cultural changes are works in progress. Building support from internal functional leaders, in addition to senior leadership, remains a significant challenge. Supply chain leaders must be ready to negotiate and influence across these lines if they are to become successful in building support for change. Finding functional support also means finding ways of financing needed investments in change initiatives. The cross-functional teams established by many firms require approvals and funding from leaders of functions outside the purview of supply chain creating pressure to justify the time and resources to be allocated to the initiatives.

Another key aspect that firms are developing as part of cultural change initiatives is interorganizational trust. While the concept can seem quite broad, there are a few aspects of trust that appear to be pervasive across different organizations as they seek to create change. One aspect is building trust and awareness of what the digital supply chain really represents. In some organizations, the digital supply chain is the natural evolution of strategies and processes, while in others digital means change that could impact associates in negative ways. In a recent executive workshop, one supply chain leader mentioned that a supply chain associate wanted to know if robots would be taking their jobs away. It is clear from this example that supply chain leaders need to think about the perceptions of their teams with respect to digital initiatives and recognize the potential of a range of emotional reactions to them. Issues concerning centralization vs. decentralization, organizational structural changes, and shifts in process ownership all represent potential impacts for associates. Building trust in the overarching strategic purpose of change is necessary to support. Trust also emerges in issues related to adopting and respecting digital process outputs. One large consumer products manufacturing firm invested millions of dollars into new digital processes and technologies to improve demand forecasts, only to have local plant managers ignore the outputs of the planning algorithms. The legacy plant managers may have mistrusted the new plans, or they may have retained loyalties to relationships built, sometimes, over decades, with local sales teams. Strategic alignment among supply chain associates and organizational change initiatives is not something one should expect to occur on blind faith. Organizational learning programs, communications plans, and campaigns, as well as pilot initiatives involving key champions and associates are needed to make change stick and enable the benefits of digital investments.

Theme Two: Data Issues are Pervasive

At a large global consumer products firm, one senior marketing executive told us that if data is the new oil, then they do not have enough refineries. This metaphor tells us a lot about how digitally oriented leaders are recognizing that firms are on the verge of becoming more data-driven and of leveraging data analytics for better and faster decisions. They are excited about the idea of introducing new data sources to help improve the resolution of analytic and predictive power. What they also speak of is the almost universal struggle to realize these visions for a large part of the problem is due to legacy system data constraints. Traditional firms commonly continue to grapple with disparate transactional system data, and while advances have been made in data quality management in recent decades, the task of aligning master data, improving accessibility of data from siloed sources, and obtaining meaningful new sources of data that can be validly modeled is still beyond the reach of many.

Theme Two: Data Issues and What Is Being Done

Data issues in large organizations are an evergreen problem. The volume, velocity, and variety of data being generated, stored, processed, and utilized continue to grow exponentially and will continue to do so in the foreseeable future. For firms that not only have legacy systems and sources, but data governance practices that are late to the game, or nonexistent, this could form a significant barrier to digital supply chain transformation. Most firms we have spoken to have undertaken some data quality initiatives and have established new data governance practices, appointed data quality champions, and have some master data management projects in flight. Objectives are being set for data accessibility and provisioning, with a mindset of providing data consumers in firms with access to the best sources of data closest to the original records. The question is, however, is it really enough? Data lakes, the current term for an idealized repository of high quality and accessible one-stop shopping for data, are not up and running in many traditional firms and if they are in production, they are often limited in scope, or quality, or type of data made available to the firms' analysts. Technology improvements may still be untapped, in cloud-based connectivity to multiple, and often unstructured, data sources, yet many supply chain leaders insist that having a fully operational and trustworthy data lake would vastly improve their speed to realize the digital supply chain benefits. If this seems to be a highly significant and high-impact challenge for firms seeking to change, what is the core issue? Our perspective is twofold. One issue pertains to creating a data culture at firms having a sense of data as a core strategic asset for the firm, thereby requiring extreme care in its handling. Digital native companies have seemingly grown up on the central importance of data to their operations where data was the engine on which they ran their companies, made decisions, and executed their business models. Traditional firms need to adopt this way of thinking and operating from the ground up and it will constitute a leadership challenge of the first order. The second issue is more practical: firms need to adopt standardized data governance practices across their firms. Clearly, this is easier to say than to execute as most supply chain leaders report. One of the key challenges to enterprise data governance is the need for the firm to act in concert, to apply governance principles across functions to enable actual data lake benefits. The driving of enterprise data governance that spans functions and allows for accessibility of customer information to the supply chain should be one of the top leadership priorities of supply chain executives.

Theme Three: What Are We Measuring?

The third theme emerging from conversations with supply chain leaders is the clear need to measure performance in new ways. It is not that the key metrics of supply chain performance have changed. Inventory turns, On-Time-In-Full, Transportation Costs, amongst others, will continue to be key performance metrics for supply chains. As we mentioned in Chapter 7, understanding how supply chain performance metrics impact the overall financial performance metrics of the firm is a wise strategy for engaging across organizational boundaries. What we are referring to in this theme, however, is more about new measures. Digital supply chain may require new metrics and new ways of interpreting the results of the metrics. For instance, one of the key objectives of the digital supply chain is to reduce costs while retaining customer satisfaction. We have heard firms say they are concerned about not sacrificing quality for the sake of efficiency, yet supply chain leaders are under constant pressure to reduce costs. This goes back to the idea of shrinking, reducing, or better managing trade-offs. Supply chain leaders are well aware of these trade-offs. Why aren't they measuring movements along these curves more often? Some firms speak of developing new, more integrated measure models. Some technological innovations, such as IoT, offer the possibilities of new data points to help gauge the life cycles of products more effectively, with greater transparency and resolution. We can only speculate on when these new data points will become part of new metrics that provide greater insights into more integrated business performance.

Metrics that offer insight into greater enterprise performance and add insight to important, yet hard to measure, factors such as human and product safety are still, it seems, on the drawing board. Metrics that support, and encourage behaviors that benefit the whole, even if individual performance is compromised, are needed if leaders are to enact integrated supply chain strategies.

Once new metrics are developed, tracked, and reported, leaders will need to demonstrate that they are paying attention to them and basing decisions on them. To bring this idea of new metrics to life, we have included a proposed set of digital supply chain metrics in the appendix of this book. The metrics are merely thought experiments, based on research conducted by the Digital Supply Chain Institute in 2017. We have not seen companies using these types of metrics yet. Perhaps a shift to measuring digital actions will lead to more rapid transformation to the digital supply chain.

Theme Four: Developing a Supply Chain Leadership Mindset

In the time just before the age of digital supply chain began to emerge and take hold, one of the world's largest consumer product brands was establishing a well-publicized supply chain leadership program. They shared their idea and successes publicly at several supply chain conferences. Articles were published about this leadership initiative, and Gartner even mentioned it in their annual ranking of supply chain excellence. The rationale for the program, as it was explained to the public was tied to business growth. The firm stated its desire to grow its business rapidly by doubling or tripling its size in global markets in the upcoming decade. At the same time, the firm realized it was not sustainable, or even possible to do so if the supply chain supporting this growth also doubled in size and cost. Recognizing this functional dilemma, that business growth must not carry with it a lockstep growth in supply chain cost is an eye-opening insight. If your finished goods utilize a natural resource as an input to production, does it mean you can simply count on doubling or tripling your use of that perishable resource to support your revenues? What if the resource required for the products was becoming scarce, perhaps shrinking, or causing less-developed parts of the world to suffer? The firm realized this approach was not sustainable.

But then how this growth could be managed in a more sustainable way? Product innovation might come into play, as well as efforts to promote and conserve natural resources. The supply chain plays a particularly important role as a majority of a firm's costs are tied up in product manufacturing, distribution, and transportation. Supply chain leaders are, in fact, accountable for a large portion of managing this dilemma. The idea of a supply chain leader dealing with this dilemma, these trade-offs, the innovation required, the problem-solving needed to overcome demands of sustainable growth has come to be called the supply chain leadership mindset. The supply chain leadership mindset concerns not simply taking orders from the upstream functions and passing products downstream. It is about thinking across boundaries. It is about looking for ways to eliminate waste. It is about finding ways of becoming more efficient without losing quality and of continuing to satisfy customers. Breaking down functional silos, improving end-to-end visibility, improving processes through innovation, communication, and problem-solving, are all part of a supply chain leadership mindset. Great supply chain leaders have always worked on reducing bullwhip, improving forecast accuracy, finding more efficient transportation networks, and differentiating supply chain designs based on segments and channels. They have always thought of ways of becoming more customer-centric, of focusing on innovation that better meets customer needs, and of working in more integrated ways with value chain partners.

They attract better and better supply chain talent and work with the suppliers of talent in productive ways. They invest in leadership development programs for their key talent while improving alignment with the goals and strategies of the firm. They realize that firms often compete with one another based on the quality and efficiency of their supply chains.

Great supply chain leaders were focused on end-to-end supply chain before the "digital" appendage appeared. They were, in short, doing all of the right things, and moving the needle on the challenges that were important. To close this volume then, we will address and summarize what is truly different about supply chain in a digital world. In a digital-, data- and technology-driven business, one that relies on a more seamless integration of the value chain, old leadership behaviors will not deliver success. The difference between traditional leadership, and digital comes down to the supply chain leadership mindset. The mindset that inspires all of your firm's associates to demonstrate the courage and have the confidence to step across the threshold of functions. It is a collective leadership. It cannot be accomplished alone. Setting your teams on the same pathway, the same journey, to a more digitally integrated approach to business performance is the essence of leading the digital supply chain.

Appendix A: Example Digital Supply Chain Metrics

Selecting appropriate metrics is crucially important as they drive the behavior that you get. Failure to identify incorrect metrics could send your organization and people into a tailspin. Here we present a recommended process for identifying a short list of Digital Supply Chain (DSC) Metrics (Digital Supply Chain Institute DSCI, 2017).

We recommend every company select at least one metric from each of these four critical areas to drive a successful DSC. Demand is so crucial and so novel to most supply chain organizations that we recommend at least two metrics. Developing a Talent Resources Strategy is also essential as it is clear that people require a variety of skills to attain DSC results. You must find people capable of capturing and analyzing data to drive better decisions. You will need more people with backgrounds in Sales and Marketing and Customer Service to drive more customer-focused growth solutions. Your metrics will shape management decisions across these areas.

Choosing new metrics, holding people accountable, and paying them for results is difficult. In particular, DSC people may sense that they cannot drive revenue. The sales team or engineers may believe that DSC people are purely operational and underestimate their efforts. If this occurs, it is a sign that you are on the right track! Navigating through this challenging process of setting new metrics and determining how to collect and use data is an integral part of the DSC as will be shown later in this document.

The DSC metrics have been divided into four areas which are critical when transforming a traditional supply chain into a digital one. Measuring for Demand, Talent, Technology, and Risk ensures that all sections of the company are fulfilling the required changes to become more demand driven, customer focused, technology savvy, and risk compliant.

Revenue Change from DSC Actions

What

Calculate the total dollar value of DSC actions that have increased revenue. These actions can include using big data to match customer demand better, stimulate sales through a "sticky" supply chain that creates advantage, better-informed product design based on DSC knowledge and local 3D manufacturing, etc. This metric will be shared (double counted) with Sales and Marketing.

Why

The DSC must shift to face the customer in a way that grows revenue. Measuring DSC-generated revenue growth is essential to focus on and will support this effort. The DSC strategy was jointly developed with Sales and Marketing.

How

Each year DSC leadership must meet with Sales and Marketing to establish the categories of actions that the DSC can take to grow revenue. Each action must be built into the budget and measured.

Revenue Increase from Platform Utilization

What

Every supply chain should grow revenue from platform partners. This revenue should be planned and measured in revenue dollars. These platform partners may be current or new suppliers or even customers.

Why

A DSC platform that connects to customers is an asset. Other companies will welcome the opportunities to access the DSC, its manufacturing, shipping, logistics, quality, and customer intimacy. Technology-enabled collaboration makes all of this possible.

How

Select a specific supply chain process that offers benefits to other vendors. Develop a revenue-sharing model that enables your company to keep a percentage of the value. Value could come from cost savings or from increased sales.

Percentage Growth in Demand due to DSC Actions

What

Calculate a target percentage increase in demand that comes from specific DSC actions. These actions could include increasing delivery speed, improving availability, offering goods and services through online channels, anticipating customer requirements, etc.

Why

This metric is similar to the Revenue Increase metric but is expressed as a percentage that enables more comfortable comparisons with other companies and previous years.

How

Percentage growth should total at least 10% of current company revenue by year three.

Demand – Process Metrics

Percentage of Perfect Orders from Automation

What

Measure the total number of perfect orders achieved through automation. Compare to total orders and to total perfect orders.

Why

Automation, done correctly, will create more perfect orders. Perfect orders create customer satisfaction. This creates more orders and revenue.

How

Count total orders, total perfect orders, and total perfect orders through automation. Integrate customer knowledge into automated systems.

Number of Days Latency in Demand Shaping/Management

What

Measure the lag time between a demand requirement and the date of fulfillment.

Why

Speed is often the biggest factor driving customer choice. Win business because of speed. This metric is increasingly important in many industries. DSC strategy will determine if this is important for your company.

How

Develop a measure of latency, track quarterly and move towards real-time tracking.

Net Promoter Score® for DSC

What

Measure the number of customers willing to recommend you as their supplier. A high score (9 or 10) is good, a low score needs to be improved.

Why

Digital Supply Chains should create customer loyalty. Customer loyalty means more revenue from existing and new customers. Net Promoter Score has been tracked by many companies but will be applied by the DSC because the DSC is focused on customer retention and growth.

How

Administer the Net Promoter Score survey to all customers and suppliers. Set the target for a score of 9 or 10. You may use the Net Promoter Score method or create your own version.

Talent – Output Metrics

Total DSC Talent Cost/ Percentage of Sales

What

Total salary and benefits costs of current and planned DSC. Calculate average pay now and compare to planned average pay.

Why

A DSC will require substantially lower people costs but average pay should increase.

How

Decide how outsourced people costs will be tracked. Include this in the calculation. Align goals for this metric with DSC Talent Strategy. DSC people costs (the total cost of people working the supply chain) divided into total sales.

Revenue Balance between Peak and Non-Peak Demand

What

Most companies have periods of high and low demand. The DSC will shift demand from peak periods to low periods. Acquire new people with skills in sales and big data analytics (e.g., data scientists) who can anticipate and shape demand through changes in availability, pricing, customization, etc.

Why

Shifting demand enables factories to operate efficiently and potentially eliminates the need for specific factories and excess inventory. Inventory can be reduced.

How

Create joint DSC/Marketing peak team to create a view of customer behavior and factory performance. Integrate big data for demand analytics.

Revenue Size of DSC Enabled Business Models Created

What

Calculate the annual revenue of a new business model created by the DSC. The single most important factor when developing new business models is to bring digital natives, marketing experts, and data scientists on board.

- A new business model could:

1. Sell DSC services to other companies that need distribution or warehousing
2. Be a "go direct" business that exists because the DSC includes sensors in products that trigger orders
3. Give products away and sell content or services
4. other

Why

Collecting new data from sensors, Internet of Things (IoT), social media and other sources will create new business opportunities for those who do it well. High-performing DSCs could become the most valuable asset of certain companies.

How

Bring people on board who can envision new ways of doing business. Invest in them and measure the results.

Revenue Increase per Supply Chain Employee due to DSC Actions

What

Measure the revenue increase per supply chain employee from DSC actions such as implementing new digital platforms, training of current employees, etc.

Why

To measure the actual impact and progress of these DSC actions into the transformation to the Digital Supply Chain. To measure the productivity per employee due to DSC transformation.

How

Make a list of all ongoing DSC actions which went through DSC transformation. Calculate the revenue increase due to the implementation of these DSC actions. Divide revenue increase by Number of employees.

Talent – Process Metrics

Total FTEs of Data Scientists/Stewards

What

Calculate the total number of data scientists and data stewards in the DSC.

Why

Data scientists and data steward skills are in great demand as they are necessary for an effective DSC. The DSC Talent Strategy will spell out the number and skill set needed. Average data and systems literacy should also increase.

How

Calculate the number of data scientists and data stewards. Set a target for the number needed as well as for the overall skill base.

Total Headcount with Sales/Marketing Expertise

What

Count the people in the supply chain with at least 3 years of experience in sales, marketing, or customer service.

Why

Front end, sales drive skills, and mindset are needed to achieve the DSC. These new people will drive a mindset/culture change.

How

Quarterly survey with targets. Comparison with DSC Talent Strategy with performance targets.

Total DSC Technology Spending

What

Add up the annual capital and expense for IT (Enterprise Software, Blockchain) and special technologies (e.g., 3D or driverless vehicles or sensors). Some judgment will be required to determine what spend is DSC spend. Building that spend baseline is important.

Why

Technology spending will go up because of the increasing amount of data, new methods of manufacturing and production, IoT, sensors, etc. Measuring and managing this spending is important. We must spend more but we must get more for what we spend.

How

Capture all the spend on technology. Include phantom servers run by the engineering department, include cloud spend that is sometimes called by the name of the internal customer. Make sure that return expectations are clear and audited.

Percentage of Sales through Direct Channels

What

Measure the percentage of business that goes directly to the customer. Not through a channel partner or reseller. This applies to B2B as well as B2C. Decide if revenue or bookings will be measured.

Why

Direct channels will deliver higher margins and more customer intimacy. This will lead to market share growth, more revenue, and higher earnings.

How

Set up a web presence that lets your customers purchase directly from you. Maintain current channels but build your own.

Technology – Process Metrics

Percentage of Revenue Facilitated by Advanced Digital Technologies

What

Measure the exact percentage of business revenue that is, or has at least some part, produced with advanced digital technologies like AI, 3D, Blockchain, IoT, etc. Measure the percentage of business revenue that is delivered by driverless cars/drones. Measure other sources of revenue that have been enabled by DSC technology.

Why

We know that 3D, driverless, and other technologies can transform the DSC. Importance of measuring, managing, and incentivizing development.

How

Collect data from factories, delivery systems, and sales or bookings. Consolidate incremental revenue and calculate percentage of total revenue.

Percentage of Time on Manual Tasks

What

Calculate the total amount of time within a certain segment of the supply chain (e.g., order to cash). Calculate the percentage of that time that requires people work as opposed to machine work.

Why

Automation is the key to reducing costs, speeding delivery of value, and improving quality. DSC automation is important.

How

Form a work team to map out existing and to-be processes. This team can also do the calculations. Be sure to employ baseline and improvement metrics so that the percentage reduction in manual work can be calculated.

Percentage of Manufacturing and Delivery Handled by Technology

What

Measure the percentage of your factory and delivery work that is automated and is not touched by human hands.

Why

The DSC will harness the power of software and machines to drive higher levels of customer satisfaction and efficiency.

How

Calculate the total number of delivery transactions made per week. Determine the percentage of those that are delivered by driverless vehicles. Determine the percent of manufacturing steps that are performed by software/machines.

Risk – Output Metrics

Percentage Change in Value of Counterfeit Goods in the Legitimate Supply Chain

What

Measure the number of counterfeits in your legitimate supply chain (legitimate defined as authorized suppliers, distributors, and retailers).

Why

Counterfeit goods are commonly found in authorized supply chains. It could be from overproduction by an authorized factory or an authorized distributor that purchases counterfeits knowingly or unknowingly.

How

Monitor the total production emerging from an authorized factory by studying raw material/ component purchases, working hours, and shipments of finished goods. Establish a mechanism for auditing distributors and retailers to establish if they have controls in place to verify that all incoming product is authentic. Sample, test, measure, and control.

Loss from Supply Chain Disruption as a percentage of Gross Revenue

What

Calculate the dollar amount of negative supply chain events as a percentage of gross revenue and track reduction against this baseline. Negative events will be defined in the DSC strategy.

Why

Business performance and compliance risks impact revenue and expenses through supply chain disruptions and losses. Measuring the reduction of risk will focus managers on reducing these problems.

How

Baseline revenue lost or expenses incurred due to negative events in the supply chain whether caused by business performance or compliance issues. Measure tangible losses such as lost sales due to supply chain disruptions.

Incremental Revenue Generated from Addressing Risk

What

Companies that excel at reducing a specific risk area can turn it into a competitive advantage to generate value for the company through increased sales, higher margins, higher valuations, increased ability to raise capital, longer-term contracts, etc.

Why

Reducing risk and converting this into more sales creates financial value. Measuring this value is essential.

How

Identify a risk area that is central to the customer. Establish a value baseline financial measurement. Track changes to this baseline.

Risk – Process Metrics

Time Lag between Capture of Critical Risk-related Data and its Inclusion in Decision Making

What

Count days between risk discovery and inclusion. Some judgment is required to determine when things are discovered and when things are decided. At the end of the performance period you should be able to calculate the average time between discovery and decision.

Why

Speed is all-important. Taking action on data that is as close to real-time as possible is essential. This risk metric will help focus people on speed of execution.

How

Identify current supply chain data sources and determine the time span between when the data first existed and when it is integrated into your risk assessment. Allocate resources to reduce the time span as needed. Measure the change reduction in days from discovery and inclusion.

Percentage of Cyber-Assessed "Connected" Suppliers

What

Calculate the total number of suppliers as a denominator. Calculate the total number that has undergone a thorough assessment of cybersecurity controls and confidential information protection programs. Divide the denominator by the number of assessments. It is important to decide what an acceptable cybersecurity assessment is and what an acceptable level of risk is.

Why

Cybersecurity and the protection of confidential information, including trade secrets, is a growing risk in the DSC. Your supplier assessment program and ongoing monitoring must cover these escalating issues. Measuring the percentage of suppliers that have been assessed is important.

How

Start by mapping all of your suppliers that are connected to any of your networks or those that receive confidential information or trade secrets from your company. Conduct assessments. As a program matures, consider weighing the percentage based on the dollar value of the supplier.

Percentage of Suppliers Classified in a Comprehensive Overall Risk Assessment

What

This examines the existence and utilization of a comprehensive risk assessment program that includes a tiered – low, medium, and high – risk rating system. Beyond that, it studies the percentage of suppliers at each risk level. Companies have traditionally done this. The DSC approach is to incorporate new sources of data, prescriptive analytics, unstructured and structured data.

Why

There is a trend in many industries towards supplier consolidation with a focus on having a smaller base of "strategic suppliers." One factor driving consolidation is that it provides more leverage and control over the supplier, thus reducing risk. Coupled with this, is the trend towards companies doing a more comprehensive and "holistic" supplier assessment of the broad range of business performance and compliance issues they face. Continuing increases in regulations will accelerate the need for comprehensive risk assessments to be conducted, with results being analyzed and implemented.

How

Establish your risk tolerance in the relevant business performance and compliance risk areas. Develop a tiered risk rating assessment and classification system of at least three levels in each of the risk areas. You may wish to aggregate this into an overall risk score. Many companies will have existing programs that can be utilized and modified as necessary to cover the enhanced risks of the DSC. Initiate the comprehensive assessment program with strategic suppliers or with those in known high-risk areas.

Appendix A. Reference

Digital Supply Chain Institute (DSCI). (2017). Digital Supply Chain Transformation Guide: Essential Metrics [White paper]. *Center for Global Enterprise.* https://www.dscinstitute.org/assets/documents/Digital-Supply-Chain-Transformation-Guide-Essential-Metrics_DSCI_Oct2.pdf.

Appendix B: Digital Supply Chain Transformation Maturity Assessment

Introduction

This tool is designed to help leaders in supply chain organizations develop a sense of where they are from an organizational perspective, as well as to begin to develop a sense of "what good looks like" in some key dimensions of the digital supply chain (Digital Supply Chain Institute DSCI, 2017). We recommend using this tool in both ways, as an actual diagnostic, to help determine focus areas, strengths, and areas for improvement, as well as to help build digital acumen.

Transformation Maturity Assessment: Survey Questions to Determine Maturity (Moss & Kurz, 2020)

Demand

This section will help you assess:

- How well your function is able to improve demand forecast accuracy
- The variety of data sources your firm utilizes to make demand decisions
- Your supply chain (SC) function's ability to utilize data to respond to rapidly changing market demands
- How deeply your SC function is involved in stimulating customer demand

The assessment questions will help you develop a better understanding of how your SC function currently interacts with and reacts to customer demand information. These are key capabilities enabling a real-time DSC (Moss & Kurz, 2020).

A SC that demonstrates a high level of performance in these categories will enable improved revenue generation and improved customer satisfaction while managing operating costs and working capital investments.

1. Currently the following sources of data are integrated into our demand planning and forecasting. (check all that apply)

   a. Internal historical data
   b. Customer data
   c. Customer's customer (consumer) data
   d. Supplier data
   e. Supplier's supplier data
   f. Social media data
   g. Relevant public data (weather, news, etc.)
   h. IoT data
   i. Consumer sentiment data
   j. Service and warranty data
   k. Competitor data

2. The following best describes how demand forecasting is done at our organization.

   a. Demand forecasting is done using available historical data and sales forecasts.
   b. Demand forecasting is done with input from various departments utilizing cross-functional data.
   c. A cross-functional consensus demand forecast is made with utilization of predictive analytics and visibility into constraints.

3. The following best describes SC's involvement in the evaluation and adjustment of our business models.

   a. SC is reactive to any changes in business models.
   b. SC is consulted in the development of new business models.
   c. SC leaders are actively involved in creating new business models.

4. The following best describes the current level of agility and adaptability of our SC:

   a. Our SC operates in a way that makes it difficult to react to changing market demands.
   b. We can rapidly respond to SC disruptions that could impact meeting customer demand.
   c. We proactively anticipate customer demand and manage our SC capacity to prevent negative impacts.

5. The following best describes the role our SC function has in stimulating and shaping demand.

   a. SC responds to demand forecasts and orders.
   b. SC is involved in consensus demand forecasting, but not integrated into demand stimulation activities.

   c. SC is fully integrated into a cross-functional team that includes product development, marketing and sales to manage our demand stimulation program.

6. If SC is involved in demand stimulation, the following sources of data are utilized. (check all that apply)

   a. Internal historical data
   b. Customer data
   c. Customer's customer (consumer) data
   d. Supplier data
   e. Supplier's supplier data
   f. Social media data
   g. Relevant public data (weather, news, etc.)
   h. IoT data
   i. Consumer sentiment data
   j. Service and warranty data
   k. Competitor data

7. The following best describes the current metrics we use in managing SC performance:

   a. We primarily use traditional SC metrics that focus on our internal performance.
   b. We are starting to test and introduce new SC metrics related to the customer.
   c. Our metrics are a blend of traditional supply metrics and new metrics that measure customer growth and satisfaction.

8. The following best describes how SC manages the trade-off between SC costs (inventory level, transportation, etc.) and customer satisfaction (example, on-time in-full).

   a. We struggle to reduce the trade-off.
   b. We are starting to improve our performance to reduce the trade-off.
   c. We are utilizing DSC activities to effectively reduce the trade-off.

9. The following best describes SC's role in collaboration with customers to generate demand:

   a. Our focus is transactional, seeking to obtain the best terms on price, delivery, and quality.
   b. We strategically develop long term relationships with key customers.
   c. We collaborate with key customers to establish data sharing and joint performance metrics.

Talent

This section will help you assess:

- The degree your talent development efforts address new digital skills
- Alignment of your job performance and compensation metrics with your DSC strategy
- The degree of cross functional collaboration between the SC and other departments
- How well your SC culture demonstrates integration behaviors
- The extent to which your SC associates are data oriented in their decision-making

The assessment questions will help you develop a better understanding of how your SC function motivates, engages, and guides the performance and commitment of your talent. The People component of the DSC transformation is a key enabler to realizing investments in technologies and processes.

A SC that demonstrates a high level of performance in these Talent categories will drive improved revenue generation and customer satisfaction while more effectively managing operating costs and working capital investments.

1. Our current personnel recruiting program supports our transformation to a DSC in the following way.

    a. We are not currently recruiting positions specific to the needs of the DSC, nor doing anything to be attractive to digital talent.
    b. We have started to position our company as being attractive to digital talent and are utilizing nontraditional methods of recruitment.
    c. Our digital talent strategy allows us to attract top the DSC talent needed to execute our DSC plan.

2. The following best describes how we develop and retain the talent needed to implement our DSC strategy.

    a. Our company's strategy for developing and retaining talent is applicable to all positions and not specific to digital talent.
    b. We recognize that developing and retaining digital talent requires a different approach and we are starting to develop one.
    c. We have a development and retention strategy that uniquely cultivates and shows commitment to building a digital community.

3. Our job performance and compensation metrics for SC personnel can best be described in the following way.

    a. SC personnel are primarily measured and compensated based on the traditional SC metrics related to quality, cost, and delivery.

b. We have started to utilize new metrics for SC personnel that are aligned with data-driven decision-making, demand stimulation and risk management.

c. SC personnel metrics are based on end-to-end SC performance and closely aligned or shared with those of marketing and sales and focused on stimulating demand and meeting customer needs.

4. Based on the priorities of our senior management and organizational structure, the following best describes today's status of cross-functional collaboration between SC and other departments in our company (such as marketing, sales, product development, human resources, finance, etc.).

a. Cross-functional collaboration, if it occurs, is sporadic, and typically facilitated in response to a specific issue.

b. We have cross-functional working groups that meet on a routine basis, however, they tend to be project specific and not linked to a broader strategic agenda.

c. SC is fully integrated into a cross-functional working group whose purpose is to drive corporate strategy and DSC performance and utilization of Artificial Intelligence/Machine Learning.

5. The following best describes the culture and behaviors that we seek to develop in SC personnel at all levels of the organization. (check all that apply):

a. Reaching across functional boundaries to seek understanding and information

b. Proactively seeking the prevention of problems at their source – irrespective of which function they originated

c. Creating and leading boundary-spanning, effective problem-solving teams

d. Placing the performance of the organization ahead of individual or unit performance

e. Demonstrating leadership that encourages collective performance

f. Effective influence and negotiation capabilities

6. Data science leaders are currently utilized in our company in the following way:

a. If we utilize data scientists, it is on a project-specific basis.

b. Data science leaders are emerging and organizing teams in our company to take advantage of algorithmic business processes.

c. Data science leaders are fully integrated into cross-functional teams that continually solve complex problems through the development and improvement of algorithms.

7. The following best describes the role of data-driven decision-making in our SC.

   a. Our SC people make decisions with limited data, based on the manual collection of historical data or by gut-instinct/ relationships.

   b. Our SC people understand how to collect and analyze quality historical data, but we are still developing the skills for determining how to apply data-driven decision-making to SC decisions.

   c. People are adept at strategically determining what SC decisions should be data-driven, identifying, collecting and analyzing the relevant data, and making data-driven decisions.

8. In our organization, the top SC executive(s) currently have influence and/or authority in the following areas:

   a. Demand planning and forecasting
   b. Capital investments in production
   c. Capital investments in technology
   d. Directly hiring and managing data analytics professionals
   e. Programs to develop and retain digital SC talent
   f. Data governance
   g. Enterprise level business model strategy
   h. Enterprise level risk management
   i. Customer satisfaction outcomes
   j. To implement transformational change programs

9. The following best describes our approach to collaboration with SC partners:

   a. Our focus is transactional, seeking to obtain the best terms on price, delivery and quality.

   b. We strategically develop long term relationships with key SC partners.

   c. We collaborate with key SC partners to establish data sharing and joint performance metrics.

Technology

This section will help you assess:

- Your SC's current use of technology speed and data latency
- The degree to which your SC is utilizing emerging relevant technologies
- How well your measurement of technology investments are aligned to digital transformation

- Your SC's relative sophistication in its cultivation of and use of data to support its digital transformation
- How well your SC collaborates with value partners through technology

The assessment questions will help you develop a better understanding of how your SC function utilizes and maximizes its investments in technology to support improved demand driven performance and risk reduction. DSC technology investments should be aligned to strategy, supported by high quality low latency data, and measured based on their performance impact.

A SC that demonstrates a high level of performance in its use of critical technologies will drive improved revenue generation and customer satisfaction while more effectively managing operating costs and working capital investments.

1. The following best describes the current role technology plays in our SC execution.

   a. We primarily use technology to facilitate traditional SC processes, related to the production and delivery or goods/services.
   b. Our technology enables performance improvements in several key SC functions.
   c. Our technology gives us a competitive advantage in end-to-end SC performance.

2. The following best describes how we evaluate the acquisition and implementation of technology to support our DSC transformation.

   a. We are not currently making technology investments specifically related to a DSC transformation.
   b. We have pilots underway to establish baseline data to identify technology investments that will support our DSC transformation.
   c. We have a rigorous review process that analyzes the ROI on technology investments and identifies those that should be scaled to support our DSC transformation.

3. The following best describes our current utilization of technology to create new business models based on DSC capabilities.

   a. We have not started to do this and/or are not sure that this is relevant to our business.
   b. We are utilizing a platform to facilitate matching demand and supply in some of the relevant areas of our business.
   c. Our SC technologies enable us to develop new business models in collaboration with our product/service development and marketing functions,

4. We have evaluated, or are in the process of evaluating the following advanced digital technologies to determine their value to our business (check all that apply):

    a. IoT
    b. 3D printing
    c. Delivery automation
    d. Blockchain
    e. AI/Machine Learning
    f. Generative design
    g. Robotics
    h. Advanced algorithms
    i. Cloud computing

5. In our SC program, our current strategic data utilization is best described in the following way:

    a. We do not have an overall strategy for data utilization and it's done on an ad hoc basis.
    b. We have projects underway to identify and integrate new internal and external data sources and improve strategic data utilization.
    c. We an established program that evaluates the use of our existing and new data to directly improve business performance and continuously seeks to find and integrate new data sources.

6. The following best describes our current utilization of algorithms to improve business performance:

    a. We primarily use algorithms to solve specific functional problems that tend to be task oriented.
    b. We use algorithms to solve problems that span functional departments and provide new business insights.
    c. We strategically use enterprise-wide algorithms leveraging predictive analytics to execute our business models.

7. The following best describes the role that data governance plays in our SC function.

    a. We do not currently have a comprehensive data governance program.
    b. Our data governance program is operational for our some of our key internal data.
    c. Our data governance program is fully operational for all of our internal data.

8. The data governance program in our SC function specifically manages the following (check all that apply).

   a. Data quality
   b. Data architecture
   c. Data development
   d. Database operations
   e. Data storage
   f. Data security (access and transfer?)
   g. Data integration and interoperability
   h. Document and content
   i. Reference and master data
   j. Data warehousing and business intelligence
   k. Meta-data

9. The following best describes how our current technology enables end-to-end SC visibility.

   a. We have visibility of some or all of our direct suppliers.
   b. We have visibility of all of our direct suppliers and some of their key subcontractors.
   c. We have visibility of all of our direct suppliers and an extensive portion of our extended SC.

Risk

This section will help you assess:

- The degree to which your SC has implemented updated risk assessment and management processes
- The relative maturity of your SC's use of data analytics to better manage risk
- The degree to which your SC is managing risk in an integrated and predictive manner
- How well you believe your SC organization manages and minimizes cyber security and confidential data breaches

The assessment questions will help you develop a better understanding of how your SC function manages, assesses, and mitigates risks due to the shift to digital. DSC risk management practices should be updated to better manage business performance and compliance risks. You can gauge if technology and data utilization is being used to shift from a reactive to a preventative control of risks.

A SC that demonstrates a high level of performance in its management of digital risk will drive improved revenue generation and customer satisfaction while more effectively managing operating costs and working capital investments.

1. The following best describes how we manage SC risks.

    a. We are primarily reactive and address problems in our SC as they arise.
    b. We have established programs that address the risks that we most commonly face and we our starting to utilize data and technology to improve efficiency.
    c. We use data analytics to seek patterns in SC risks and related negative impacts and adjust our risk management program to reduce or prevent occurrence.

2. We have implemented a proactive risk management program for the following types of SC performance risks. (check all that apply)

    a. On-time delivery
    b. In-full delivery
    c. Quality of goods and services received
    d. Transportation costs
    e. Transportation network failures
    f. Product or service cost overruns
    g. SC disruption
    h. Supplier dependency

3. We have implemented a pro-active risk management program for the following types of SC compliance risks. (check all that apply)

    a. Regulatory compliance
    b. Cybersecurity
    c. Data privacy
    d. Labor compliance
    e. Environmental compliance
    f. Counterfeit goods/materials
    g. Product integrity and security
    h. Loss of trade secrets/confidential information
    i. Corruption

4. The following best describes how we utilize our risk management program to gain a competitive advantage in the marketplace.

    a. Our risk management program is focused on mitigating our most common SC risks.
    b. We have identified specific risk areas where we can excel and are starting to implement programs to do so.
    c. We are recognized for having active risk management programs that make us a top-tier performer in the selected risk areas.

5. The following best describes how we monitor the evolving risk landscape and its impact on our SC continuity.

   a. We informally collect information through our existing relationships and relevant publicly available sources.

   b. We are starting to use analytics to gather and analyze data to monitor the risk areas that are most important to our business.

   c. Our monitoring program uses predictive analytics to gather and analyze structured and unstructured data to generate alerts based on the risk tolerance we have established.

6. We currently do the following to minimize cybersecurity risk and the related loss of confidential information *inside our organization.* (check all that apply)

   a. Provide employees with policies
   b. Provide employees with procedures
   c. Train employees
   d. Classify the value of information
   e. Clearly mark information that is confidential or a trade secret
   f. Maintain restrictive electronic and physical access controls
   g. Monitoring of access, use and transfer of critical confidential information
   h. Regular evaluation, benchmarking, and improvement of internal cybersecurity and confidential information protection program

7. We currently do the following to minimize cybersecurity risk and the related loss of confidential information *with companies in our SC.* (check all that apply)

   a. Provide SC partners with policies
   b. Provide SC partners with procedures
   c. Train SC partners
   d. Classify the value of information shared with SC partners
   e. Clearly mark shared information that is confidential or a trade secret
   f. Require that they maintain restrictive electronic and physical access controls
   g. Monitoring their use and transfer of critical confidential information
   h. Regular evaluation, benchmarking, and improvement of key SC partner cybersecurity and confidential information protection program

Outside In

One of the most fundamental shifts needed to transform to a DSC is reorienting from an internal focus to a customer focus. To do this effectively means engaging your customers and your suppliers in assessing your SC performance. It also means broad internal engagement. We recommend distributing the Transformation Maturity Assessment to all your SC staff, as well as selected customer facing sales and marketing, IT, and finance staff. In addition, we suggest asking at least five customers and five suppliers the questions below. Ideally, responses would be confidentially collected by a third party.

1. How well does our company's SC anticipate and match demand? (Select One)

    a. One of the very best (4 Points)
    b. Better than most (3 Points)
    c. About average (2 Points)
    d. Worse than most (1 Point)

2. How well does our SC staff collaborate with your company for our mutual benefit? (Select One)

    a. One of the very best (4 Point)
    b. Better than most (3 Points)
    c. About average (2 Points)
    d. Worse than most (1 Point)

3. How would you assess the state of our technology and its capabilities? (Select One)

    a. One of the very best (4 Point)
    b. Better than most (3 Points)
    c. About average (2 Points)
    d. Worse than most (1 Point)

4. How well do you think we manage business performance and compliance risks? (Select One)

    a. One of the very best (4 Point)
    b. Better than most (3 Points)
    c. About average (2 Points)
    d. Worse than most (1 Point)

DSC Transformation Summary Maturity Scale

This scale is applicable to manufacturing and service industries. It seeks to measure the maturity of the transformation and to provide insight into how an organization can prioritize areas for improvement that will accelerate the transformation.

Execution will differ depending on whether your business is historically considered a service business or a product business. Ultimately, we believe that all companies do have DSC and will need to embrace a platform business model to some extent.

	1	2	3
Demand	We have not started to integrate demand management or stimulation into our SC.	Performance metrics specifically include demand stimulation, demand shaping, and demand management and we have started implementation.	Our SC program is aligned with the Customer-centric models. Our demand sensing and stimulation program enables us to generate additional revenue through improved demand visibility and the ability to satisfy the demand. We have a program to review and improve our performance against DSC metrics and benchmarks.
Talent	Our staffing, job performance metrics, and leadership development plans do not consider DSC transformation.	DSC and collaboration are integrated in our staffing, job performance metrics, and leadership development plans. We have started Implementation.	Senior leadership shows clear commitment to the principles of DSC and appropriate performance metrics are fully integrated into how we hire, develop, and compensate people. The effectiveness of cross-functional collaboration and collaboration with value-chain partners is measured. SC leadership is

	1	2	3
			heavily involved in corporate strategy and has appropriate decision-making authority.
Technology	Our technology implementation plans are not yet specifically linked to our DSC strategy.	DSC and relevant use of platform business are central to our technology strategy and we have started implementation.	We strategically utilize digital technology to improve SC performance. We continually evaluate application of new technologies and data sources and integrate as appropriate. We utilize data and analytics to effectively understand past performance and predict future demand and risks.
Risk	We have not started to specifically analyze risk mitigation opportunities and new risks of the DSC.	Our risk assessment includes an evaluation of new DSC risks as well as how DSC can help manage SC risks. We have started implementation of programs to improve DSC risk management internally and with the companies in our value chain.	We use data to reduce business performance and compliance risk through predictive analytics, with a specific focus on cybersecurity and protection of confidential information. We have a risk management strategy that segments risks into those we manage and those we seek to excel at to gain a competitive advantage.

References

Digital Supply Chain Institute (DSCI) (2017). Digital Supply Chain Transformation Guide: Essential Metrics [White paper]. *Center for Global Enterprise.* https://www.dscinstitute.org/assets/documents/Digital-Supply-Chain-Transformation-Guide-Essential-Metrics_DSCI_Oct2.pdf.

Moss, C., & Kurz, D. (2020). *Digital Supply Chain Transformation Maturity Assessment V2.* [Unpublished manuscript].

Glossary

- 3D Printing: 3D printing (also known as additive, digital, and rapid manufacturing) is a process of making a physical object from a three-dimensional digital model, typically by laying down many thin layers of a material in succession. Unlike traditional ("subtractive") manufacturing processes, 3D printing technology allows users to build highly complex products from a large variety of materials (e.g., plastic, metal, ceramic, sandstone, resin, biomaterial, and food substances) while demanding little to no retooling from work order to work order, or product to product. This flexibility allows for unparalleled levels of customization, to the point where each printed unit can be an entirely new product, i.e., one of a kind. Instead, local fabrication, which can be viewed as an intermediary or parallel phase, could prove to be more feasible. On-demand 3D printing service providers carry out a range of 3D printing-related services from design through to manufacturing.
- Adaptive Neuro-Fuzzy Inference System (ANFIS): Adaptive Neuro-Fuzzy Inference System is a combination between neural networks and fuzzy logic is to benefit from the advantages of both methodologies. Fuzzy logic uses a combination of mathematical predictive power and human subjectivity to create the best model possible. While this would not be considered "machine learning" because of the human interactivity component, an extension of fuzzy logic has limited human subjectivity and added artificial neural network predictive power to the fuzzy logic schema.
- Advanced Analytics: Advanced Analytics is the autonomous or semiautonomous examination of data or content using sophisticated techniques and tools, typically beyond those of traditional business intelligence (BI), to discover deeper insights, make predictions, or generate recommendations. Advanced analytic techniques include those such as data/text mining, machine learning, pattern matching, forecasting, visualization, semantic analysis, sentiment analysis, network and cluster analysis, multivariate statistics, graph analysis, simulation, complex event processing, and neural networks.

- Advanced images and voice recognition: Voice recognition and synthesis technology are picking up where bar codes left off, promising to bring huge improvements to supply chains. In the typical voice technology system, supply chain workers wear a headset and microphone connected to a mobile computer that they carry with them. The mobile computer communicates wirelessly with a computer server running a supply chain management software package.
- Artificial intelligence (AI): AI applies advanced analysis and logic-based techniques, including machine learning, to interpret events, support and automate decisions, and take actions.
- Alignment: Strategic management theory suggests that proper internal and external alignment throughout the supply chain, among all the functional areas such as logistics, marketing, and finance, will help companies achieve their competitive advantages.
- Analytics maturity curve: Gartner's Analytics Maturity Curve breaks down the past, present, and future of analytics into five phases. From descriptive to predictive to cognitive and everything in between.
- Artificial neural networks (ANN): ANN is an emerging AI technology, which is put forward based on the modern biology research achievements of human brain tissue. The function of ANN is to give an output pattern when presented with an input pattern. ANN is a powerful technique for solving complex approximation and classification problems due to their high generalization capability, robust design, and ability to handle incomplete data.
- ARIMA (autoregressive integrated moving average demand forecasts): Mathematical models of supply chains provide managerial insights about supply chain dynamics. For instance, these models have led to an understanding of the Bullwhip effect. One such model is ARIMA models are typically fitted to time series data either to better understand the data or to predict future points in the series (forecasting). ARIMA models are applied in some cases where data show evidence of non-stationarity, where an initial differencing step (corresponding to the "integrated" part of the model) can be applied one or more times to eliminate the nonstationarity.
- Autonomous Systems: Autonomous systems take over the work automatically. The use of technologies such as robots and drones are spreading rapidly in supply chains. Autonomous systems are used to improve predictive maintenance, often in combination with sensors, and even to take action. In warehouses, robots are employed to assist humans in selecting items and helping to carry and pack them, track inventory and inventory levels. In addition, cobots, which are lighter mobile robots that can perform tasks with and around humans.

- Big data: Big data is high-volume, high-velocity, and/or high-variety information assets that demand cost-effective, innovative forms of information processing that enable enhanced insight, decision-making, and process automation.
- Big data analytics: Big data analytics is the use of advanced analytic techniques against very large, diverse data sets that include structured, semi-structured, and unstructured data, from different sources, and in different sizes from terabytes to zettabytes.
- Black swans: A black swan is an unpredictable event that is beyond what is normally expected of a situation and has potentially severe consequences. Black swan events are characterized by their extreme rarity, severe impact, and the widespread insistence they were obvious in hindsight.
- Blockchain: A blockchain is an expanding list of cryptographically signed, irrevocable transactional records shared by all participants in a network. Each record contains a time stamp and reference links to previous transactions. With this information, anyone with access rights can trace back a transactional event, at any point in its history, belonging to any participant.
- Business Analytics: Business analytics is comprised of solutions used to build analysis models and simulations to create scenarios, understand realities, and predict future states. Business analytics includes data mining, predictive analytics, applied analytics and statistics, and is delivered as an application suitable for a business user.
- Bullwhip effect: The bullwhip effect is a distribution channel phenomenon in which demand forecasts yield supply chain inefficiencies. It refers to increasing swings in inventory in response to shifts in consumer demand as one moves further up the supply chain.
- Cloud computing is a style of computing in which scalable and elastic IT-enabled capabilities are delivered as a service using internet technologies.
- Cloud technologies: Given the dynamic and complex nature of the supply chain, organizations may seek flexibility in the type of cloud services required. Cloud services are typically offered in three ways:

  o Infrastructure as a Service (IaaS): The most basic category of cloud computing services. A concept of renting rather than buying. With IaaS, the organization rents IT infrastructure – servers and virtual machines, storage, networks, operating systems – from a cloud provider on a pay-as-you-go basis.
  o Platform as a Service (PaaS): PaaS supplies an on-demand environment for developing, testing, delivering, hosting, and managing software applications. The provider of the service

manages the routine maintenance of the infrastructure, but users of the service write and upload their code to the provider.

o Software as a Service (SaaS): A method for delivering software applications over the internet. With SaaS, cloud providers host and manage the software application and underlying infrastructure and handle any maintenance, such as software upgrades and security patching. Users connect to the application over the internet – usually with a web browser on their phone, tablet, or PC.

- Cognitive computing: Cognitive computing is often used to indicate systems such as Google DeepMind's AlphaGo or IBM's Watson that can reason and understand at a high order similar to human thinking. Generally speaking, cognitive computing is a subset of AI that uses multiple AI technologies to produce what we recognize as thinking.
- Data governance: Data governance is the specification of decision rights and an accountability framework to ensure the appropriate behavior in the valuation, creation, consumption, and control of data and analytics.
- Data lake: A data lake is a centralized data storing repository. It stores unstructured and structured data of any scale. Data lakes store data of any size, shape, and speed, and perform processing and analytics across platforms and languages. They remove the complexities of ingesting and storing data while accelerating batch, streaming, and interactive analytics. There is a stark difference between data lakes and data warehouses. Data lakes support structured, unstructured, and raw data, whereas warehouses only support structured and processed data. Data warehouses tend to be rigid and large. Data lakes are agile and low cost.
- Data quality: Data quality tools are the processes and technologies for identifying, understanding, and correcting flaws in data that support effective information governance across operational business processes and decision-making. The packaged tools available include a range of critical functions, such as profiling, parsing, standardization, cleansing, matching, enrichment, and monitoring.
- Data warehouses: A data warehouse is a storage architecture designed to hold data extracted from transaction systems, operational data stores, and external sources. The warehouse then combines that data in an aggregate summary form suitable for enterprise-wide data analysis and reporting for predefined business needs. A data warehouse contains data arranged into abstracted subject areas with time-variant versions of the same records, with an appropriate level of data grain or detail to make it useful across two or more different types of analyses most often deployed with

tendencies to third normal form. A data mart contains similarly time-variant and subject-oriented data, but with relationships implying dimensional use of data wherein facts are distinctly separate from dimension data, thus making them more appropriate for single categories of analysis.

- Digital twins: A digital twin is a digital representation of a real-world entity or system. Digital twins will include all aspects of the product, including its parts list, simulation and analysis results, materials, manufacturing requirements, and quality data. Once the product is disseminated to users, data will continue to be collected with the goal of using field performance to enhance future models. The digital twin gathers a number of individual technologies related to the product, from computer-aided data to 3D-printed prototypes. These technologies are connected to the organization's ERP system so that marketing and sales information is also available. Data from multiple digital twins can be aggregated for a composite view across a number of real-world entities, such as a power plant or a city, and their related processes.
- Edge computing is part of a distributed computing topology where information processing is located close to the edge, where things and people produce or consume that information.
- Enterprise resource planning (ERP): ERP is defined as the ability to deliver an integrated suite of business applications. ERP tools share a common process and data model, covering broad and deep operational end-to-end processes, such as those found in finance, HR, distribution, manufacturing, service, and the supply chain.
- Extraction, Transformation and Loading (ETL): ETL is a type of data integration that refers to the three steps (extract, transform, load) used to blend data from multiple sources. During this process, data is taken (extracted) from a source system, converted (transformed) into a format that can be analyzed, and stored (loaded) into a data warehouse or other system.
- Generative design: Generative design is a design exploration process. Designers input design goals into the generative design software, along with parameters such as performance or spatial requirements, materials, manufacturing methods, and cost constraints. The software explores all the possible permutations of a solution, quickly generating design alternatives. It tests and learns from each iteration what works and what does not.
- Internet of Things (IoT): IoT is the network of physical objects that contain embedded technology such as RFID sensors to communicate with the external environment. This allows real-time visibility of inventory and has increased the speed of tracking and the accuracy of product forecasting and planning.

- Immersive technologies: Immersive technologies are one of the leading assistance systems in the supply chain space. It changes the way people perceive the world by taking users beyond 2D viewing. This is completed by augmenting the real world with virtual objects or by immersing users in a 3D virtual environment. The most advanced systems enable full freedom of movement. Users can walk around virtual objects in the real world or walk through a virtual world they can see, hear, touch, and feel. There are three types of technologies in this space:

  o Virtual Reality (VR) provides a computer-generated 3D environment that surrounds users and responds to their actions in a natural way. Gesture recognition and handheld controllers provide hand and body tracking, and touch-sensitive feedback may be incorporated.
  o Augmented Reality (AR) is the real time use of information in the form of text, graphics, video and other virtual enhancements integrated with real-world objects. This overlaying of virtual world elements on a real-world background differentiates AR from VR. AR aims to enhance users' interactions with the real physical environment, rather than separating them from it.
  o Mixed Reality (MR) takes the immersive experience to the next level by sensing objects in the real world. It transforms those objects with virtual augmentations or by placing virtual objects in space users can explore in 3D. Users may interact with digital and real-world objects while maintaining their presence in the physical world.

- Machine Learning: A crucial development in the field of analytics is machine learning. Machine learning uses algorithms to make predictions by analyzing large amounts of data. The unique aspect of machine learning is the capability to learn and adjust the analysis by observing additional data; the more data fed through the algorithms, the more accurate the predictions become. Advanced machine learning algorithms are composed of many technologies, such as deep learning, artificial neural networks, and natural language processing.
- Natural Language Processing (NLP): NLP technology involves the ability to turn text or audio speech into encoded, structured information, based on an appropriate ontology. The structured data may be used simply to classify a document or may be used to identify products, procedures, attributes, and people.
- Predictive Analytics: While descriptive analytics focus primarily on the past and present, predictive analytics uses data-driven predictions to better understand potential future outcomes.

Predictive analytics lean heavily on data mining and machine learning algorithms to learn from data and to forecast future outcomes based on identified patterns. Advanced predictive tools enhance data generated from sources such as sensors and external sources. Prediction is key to business value delivered by supply chain platforms; the competitive advantage to be gained from predictive analytics is derived from the forward-looking insights it generates, allowing supply chain managers to be more proactive in decision making and planning.

- Prescriptive Analytics: Prescriptive analytics goes beyond descriptive and predictive analytics by recommending actions. Using simulation models and optimization algorithms, prescriptive analytics quantify the results of various decision paths based on expected outcomes. This level of analytics addresses "what if" scenarios and focuses on future uncertainty. Prescriptive Analytics is a form of advanced analytics that examines data or content to answer the question "What should be done?" and is characterized by techniques such as graph analysis, simulation, complex event processing, neural networks, recommendation engines, heuristics, and machine learning.

- Real-time Analytics: Real-time analytics is the discipline that applies logic and mathematics to data to provide insights for making better decisions quickly. For some supply chain use cases, real time simply means the analytics is completed within a few seconds or minutes after the arrival of new data. On-demand real-time analytics waits for users or systems to request a query and then delivers the analytic results. Continuous real-time analytics is more proactive and alerts users or triggers responses as events happen.

- Radio Frequency Identification (RFID): RFID refers to an automated data collection technology that uses radio frequency waves to transfer data between a reader and a tag to identify, track, and locate the tagged item. There are two basic categories of tags used in supply chains: passive and battery-enabled.

- Robotics: In warehouses, robots are employed to assist humans in selecting items and helping to carry and pack them. They also track inventory and inventory levels. Lighter and mobile robots also known as cobots are used in supply chains for performing tasks with and around humans.

- Unstructured Data: In the modern world of big data, unstructured data is the most abundant. It's so prolific because unstructured data could be anything: media, imaging, audio, sensor data, text data, and much more. *Unstructured* simply means that it is datasets (typical large collections of files) that aren't stored in a structured database format. Unstructured data has an internal structure, but it's not predefined through data models. It might be human generated, or machine generated in a textual or a non-textual format.

- Wearable Applications: Wearable applications are a diverse group of endpoint devices connecting humans to the IoT through sensors. Data is accessed via wearables – through portable computer systems such as smart watches or activity trackers that display context-sensitive information or provide instructions. Examples of wearable devices head-mounted displays for remote expert guidance, visual instructions, or hands-free training.

Index

Printed in the United States
By Bookmasters